Praise for *The Big Story*

I think we need to be reminded every single day that we are part of a Bigger Story, part of something greater than ourselves, and that each of our stories matter—a great deal. To be reminded of that truth is to live in Hope. *The Big Story* gives the reader that gift of Hope.

> —**SALLY LLOYD-JONES**, author of *The Jesus Storybook Bible* and
> *Thoughts to Make Your Heart Sing*

A good story needs a good teller. And Justin Buzzard fits that bill. He not only explains the Bible's dynamic plot, but draws us persuasively into the greatest story ever told—with arresting images and vivid analogies that connect our stories to The Big Story. In the process, you'll find yourself being swept into a world you didn't make and therefore can't unmake. It's good news in a bad news world.

> —**MICHAEL HORTON**, professor of theology, Westminster Seminary
> California, cohost of the White Horse Inn, and author of *Pilgrim
> Theology: Core Doctrines for Christ's Disciples*

I cannot overemphasize the desperate need to retell the amazing storyline of the Bible and our place in that story to new generations. Without this, it is far too easy to drift into unfortunate pathways and dead ends that are sadly missing the beauty of the story God has for us. I am very thankful for Justin's book, which gives direction to a world in need of understanding the true way, and the true story.

> —**DAN KIMBALL**, pastor, Vintage Faith Church, author of
> *They Like Jesus but Not The Church*

The overarching theme of Scripture, of course, is the life of Jesus. What makes this new book by Justin Buzzard so good is that it not only highlights the incredible story of Scripture, but it shows us how our story fits neatly in Jesus' story. As we understand Jesus' story, and our place in it, we are motivated to join God on mission, sharing Jesus' story with the world. This book is a great asset to God's kingdom work.

> —**ED STETZER**, president of LifeWay Research

You don't need to read this entire book. Just try the first few pages. I predict you'll have a hard time putting it down. Justin Buzzard knows the Greatest Story well, and he knows how to retell it in a way that can be compelling to those who have never heard it and refreshing to those of us who need to hear it again and again. Try it and see.

> —**JUSTIN TAYLOR**, coauthor, *The Final Days of Jesus,*
> blogger, "Between Two Worlds"

D0061875

There are great stories and great storytellers. But there is nothing like "The Big Story". Justin Buzzard captures the compelling drama of the Bible in a way that demands your attention, and ultimately, your allegiance. If you have been skeptical about the message of the Bible, or if you have found its story confusing, sit down with this book immediately. You will quickly see how your story needs to intersect with "The Big Story"."

—**J. PAUL NYQUIST**, Ph.D., president of Moody Bible Institute

Fundamental to human existence is the question of identity and purpose. Who am I? Why am I here? Justin Buzzard, in his book, *The Big Story*, helps us to find our place in the unfolding drama of life. As the narrative unfolds, get ready to be compellingly called on stage to be a character in the adventure that Buzzard calls the "Big Story".

—**BRYAN LORITTS**, lead pastor, Fellowship Memphis and
author of *A Cross-Shaped Gospel*

"Epic" is too small a word for the story of God's work in this world. Justin shares the one big story so you can see the scarlet thread of Jesus' atoning sacrifice through the tapestry of the Bible. Where does this scarlet thread intersect *your* life? Rejoice as you read in *The Big Story* that you're not the center of the universe, and worship Jesus as you learn more about our Savior who set the stars in place and numbered the hairs on your head.

—**GLORIA FURMAN**, author of *Glimpses of Grace*

Is this Bible a book of rules? Is it an instruction manual for Christians? I was taught both growing up in a nominally Christian family. What I would later discover is that the Bible was neither of those things. Rather, the Bible is God's grand narrative of humanity's continued desire to carve their own path, and God's overwhelming love and continued intervention when our way finally fails us.

The Bible is the story of God's great love for His creation, what He once called "very good." And this incredible story culminates in the coming of Jesus, and our being invited, through Him, to find our true place in His story. My friend Justin captures this with earnestness, care, and clarity as he paints for us the beautiful picture of what God is doing in the world, and where we find our place in His story.

—**LEONCE CRUMP II**, lead elder, Renovation Church

The story of the gospel is the most compelling aspect of our faith, and this book winsomely captures the heart of what makes it so attractive. It addresses life's greatest struggles and longings with rock-solid truth conveyed through God's redemption narrative in the Bible.

—**MATT CARTER**, pastor of preaching and vision at the Austin Stone
Community Church and coauthor of *The Real Win: A Man's Quest for
Authentic Success*

THE BIG STORY

HOW THE BIBLE MAKES SENSE OUT OF LIFE

JUSTIN BUZZARD

MOODY PUBLISHERS

CHICAGO

All Scripture quotations, unless otherwise indicated, are taken from *The Holy Bible, English Standard Version.* Copyright © 2000, 2001 by Crossway Bibles, a division of Good News Publishers. Used by permission. All rights reserved.

Scripture quotations marked KJV are taken from the King James Version.

Scripture quotations marked NIV are taken from the Holy Bible, New International Version®, NIV®. Copyright © 1973, 1978, 1984 by Biblica, Inc.™ Used by permission of Zondervan. All rights reserved worldwide. www.zondervan. com. The "NIV" and "New International Version" are trademarks registered in the United States Patent and Trademark Office by Biblica, Inc.™

Emphasis in Scripture is the author's.

Edited by Bailey Utecht

Cover design: Design Corps

Cover image: iStock #13789461/#16190419

Interior design: Smartt Guys design

ISBN: 978-0-8024-0857-0

We hope you enjoy this book from Moody Publishers. Our goal is to provide high-quality, thought-provoking books and products that connect truth to your real needs and challenges. For more information on other books and products written and produced from a biblical perspective, go to www.moodypublishers.com or write to:

Moody Publishers
820 N. LaSalle Boulevard
Chicago, IL 60610

1 3 5 7 9 10 8 6 4 2

Printed in the United States of America

This book is dedicated to my three sons: Cru, Hudson, and Gus. Buzzard boys, I love you, like you, and enjoy you so much. Being your dad is a nonstop adventure. My prayer for all three of you is that you grow up to be brave and happy men who live in the thick of this Big Story and cause a ruckus on this planet.

CONTENTS

Introduction 9

1. Jesus 15

2. Act 1: God. 25

3. Act 2: Creation 45

4. Act 3: Rebellion. 63

5. Act 4: Rescue 87

6. Intermission 111

7. Act 5: Home 123

8. Life 145

Appendix: How to Retell Other People's Stories
with the Big Story 167

Notes. 171

Special Thanks. 179

*"Stories are how we remember;
we tend to forget lists and bullet points."*
—Robert McKee[1]

· · ·

INTRODUCTION

What *is your story?*

In 2011 I moved my wife and three sons to Silicon Valley to pursue a dream. I wanted to start a new church[2] that would engage my city with the gospel (the story of the Bible) in a new way. The day we moved, I had just three people committed to my dream and just three thousand dollars in the church bank account. I'd never felt so excited or so scared. It was a move of faith. I had no guarantees. But it all felt so right, like the next chapter in the story that God was writing for my life.

I've always sensed that my life is part of a bigger story. It's the times when I've forgotten this bigger story that I've felt the most lost in life. Life is full of seasons. Whether I've been navigating a season of excitement or suffering, it's always been my grip on what I call the "Big Story," or the Big Story's grip on me, that has helped me make sense of the ups and downs of life. Years ago I read a quote that put this perfectly:

> The same impulse that makes us want our books to have a plot makes us want our lives to have a plot. We need to feel that we are getting somewhere, making progress. There is something in us that is not satisfied with a merely psychological explanation of our lives. It doesn't do justice to our conviction that we are on some kind of journey or quest, that there must be some deeper meaning to our lives than whether we feel good about ourselves. Only people who have lost the sense of adventure, mystery, and romance worry about their self-esteem. And at that point what they need is not a good therapist, but a good story. Or more precisely, the central question for us should not be, "What personality dynamics explain my behavior?" but rather, "What sort of story am I in?"[3]

What sort of story am I in? This is the question I've been asking all my life. This is the question I believe everyone in my city is asking and needs an answer to. This is the question everyone on the planet needs to wrestle with.

What sort of story are you in?

Questions precede answers. There's no use talking about answers unless we first get our questions right. You and I have our question: *What sort of story are we in?* Throughout the ages people have given many different answers to this question. Your neighbors, coworkers, and local bookstore all offer different answers to our question. If you filled the room you're in right now with a mixture of both atheists and deeply religious people, you'd hear fifty different stories from all these people. But they all believe the story that they think makes sense out of their lives.

My conviction is that only one story is big enough to adequately answer this question, to explain all the beauty and all the brokenness we see in this world, to make sense of our desires, dreams, and disappointments. I've looked at the other answers to this question, the other stories that are out there, but they all felt too small. I don't know what people believe in your town or city, but my city is a diverse mix of Buddhists, Atheists, Sikhs, Hindus, Christians, Muslims, Mormons, Jews, and Confused (people who aren't sure what they believe). My conclusion is that these other worldviews don't make complete sense of this world. Their plots have too many gaps, and their answers are too shallow for our deepest pain, deepest desires, and deepest questions.

The Big Story, the story we need, is the old and ongoing story of the Bible. The Bible is a collection of ancient manuscripts written over fifteen hundred years by over forty different authors that tells one big story about God and people. It's a strange story. It's a good story. It's a complicated and challenging story. It's a thrilling story. It's a story that's still moving, a story in which you play an important part. It, I think, is the only story big enough to make sense out of everything you've been through and everything you and the people you love will face in the future.

Let me be up front about how wild this story is. I'm going to spend the next eight chapters walking you through the major movements in this old, yet living book called the Bible, which is about:

the One Story of God's incomprehensible, outrageous acts of redemption, the stories of a God gathering a people for His name. Here in its pages appear fierce and unlikely heroes, terrifying battles, pilloried prophets, resistant saints, miraculous healings, a foot-washing King, a bloodied God on a cross, a hollow tomb, the final wrath and glory judgment, and a denouement that ends more miraculously than anything we could imagine: the coming of a new city with open gates and a purified people now called sons and daughters who, needing no other light, will enter and walk by the light of the Lamb.

Not everyone will be there. It is not a safe or simple story. Yet the story is for all of us to hear and heed. We are invited into these pages, not as editors with red pens in hand, but as supplicants seeking understanding and truth. We are invited to live into this narrative, but not to rewrite it, either to gut it of its offense or to reshape it for short attention spans and better sales.[4]

Even if you don't believe in God and the Bible as I do, I invite you to listen to this story, to live into it a little, and examine if it does or doesn't make sense of things for you. Have you ever watched one of those movies that begins in the middle of the story and then goes back to the beginning, to the start of the story? That's what I'm about to do. We're going to start in the middle of the story with the greatest disruption you could ever experience in your life: Jesus. Then we'll go back to the beginning and work our way, front to back, through this Big Story and its five main acts: God, Creation, Rebellion, Rescue, Home (and a short, important intermission). And finally the epilogue of the story: Life, the time of the story in which we now live, a time that's in between the fourth act (Rescue) and the fifth act (Home).

Whether or not you're someone who believes in prayer, I invite you to pray a simple prayer before you read this book. I'm writing this book right now believing that you'll agree to do this, that you'll pray before you read. I believe prayer changes things. I believe when you pray you're talking to a God who hears you and cares about you. Prayer can dramatically change the whole experience of writing and reading a book. I have been praying for all of you who are reading this, and now it's your turn:

God, speak to me as I read this book. Make Yourself more real to me. Do something new in my life and through my life.

That was easy. Now you may turn the page.

P.S. If you would like to interact with me while reading this book, you can contact me through Twitter (@JustinBuzzard), and I'll do my best to respond to any messages.

"I wanted movement and not a calm course of existence. I wanted excitement and danger and a chance to sacrifice myself for my love."

—Leo Tolstoy[1]

• • •

"All our human stories of heroes, monsters, journeys, and sacrifice give voice to our universal quest for identity, purpose, and deliverance. Instead of competing with God's story, these stories gesture toward it."

—Leslie Leyland Fields[2]

• • •

"The whole story of the world—and of how we fit into it—is most clearly understood through a careful, direct look at the story of Jesus . . . how beautifully his life makes sense of ours."

—Tim Keller[3]

• • •

1

JESUS

Recently I was invited by an old friend to join him and six other men and climb Mount Rainier outside of Seattle, Washington—all 14,410 feet of it. I flew north and joined them, strapped on my crampons and backpack, hoisted my ice axe, and started climbing.

It was the hardest thing I have ever done.

This mountain is covered in ice, blanketed in glaciers, with crevasses hundreds of feet deep. Some people might try to convince you those are called *crevices*, but I'm telling you, those on Mount Rainier are *crevasses,* and they will kill a man. Toting dozens of pounds of clothing and gear up that mountain was exhausting, petrifying, and thrilling.

The main reason my old friend asked me to join him and the other guys on the climb was to talk about Jesus. See, these other guys don't know Jesus, and he wanted me to tell them about Him. My old friend is a former Marine and he figured the best place to have good conversation about Jesus with a bunch of tough guys was on top of a freezing mountain. So, when I wasn't terrified of falling into a crevasse and dying, I told these men what I know about Jesus.

Jesus?

Everyone has a reaction to Jesus. He isn't someone who can be ignored. Love Him or hate Him, you must respond to Him.

Here are some examples of how a few famous people thought of Jesus.

"I love the idea of the teachings of Jesus Christ and the beautiful stories about it, which I loved in Sunday school and I collected all the little stickers and put them in my book. But the reality is that organized religion doesn't seem to work. It turns people into hateful lemmings and it's not really compassionate."[4] —*Elton John*

"The example of Jesus suffering is a factor in the composition of my un-dying faith in non-violence. What then does Jesus mean to me? To me, He was one of the greatest teachers humanity has ever had."[5] —*Mahatma Gandhi*

"Christianity will go. It will vanish and shrink. I needn't argue with that; I'm right and I will be proved right. We're more popular than Jesus now; I don't know which will go first—rock 'n' roll or Christianity. Jesus was all right but his disciples were thick and ordinary."[6] —*John Lennon*

"I'm a Muslim, but I think Jesus would have a drink with me. He would be cool. He would talk to me."[7] —*Mike Tyson*

So Jesus is a good idea even if His followers aren't so great. Or maybe He is a fantastic example and a dynamic teacher. It could be that He is just a passing fad who will fade away. (It seems like two thousand years of popularity indicate that's not the case.) Or maybe, regardless of our worldview, Jesus is a cool guy to hang out with. That's what these guys thought.

How do *you* react to Jesus? We are all looking for someone or something to follow. What do you think about the idea of following Jesus?

Disturbance

The reason Jesus elicits such powerful reactions is simple and profound: Jesus disturbs our lives. To disturb means "to interfere with the normal arrangement."[8] People *have* to respond to Jesus because He shows up in their lives and starts to interfere. Jesus doesn't leave things as they are; He both attracts people to Himself and meddles with their lives.

The Bible contains four biographies (also called "Gospels") about the life of Jesus. In one of those biographies, the book of Mark, we see Jesus doing His disturbing work of simultaneously attracting people to Himself and meddling with their lives. Feel free to read this part of the Bible as I've printed it below, or get your hands on a Bible[9] and read these verses—and all following verses—from the pages of your own Bible (that way you can better explore the surrounding context).

Now after John was arrested, Jesus came into Galilee, proclaiming the gospel of God, and saying, "The time is fulfilled, and the kingdom of God is at hand; repent and believe in the gospel."

Passing alongside the Sea of Galilee, he saw Simon and Andrew the brother of Simon casting a net into the sea, for they were fishermen. And Jesus said to them, "Follow me, and I will make you become fishers of men." And immediately they left their nets and followed him. And going on a little farther, he saw James the son of Zebedee and John his brother, who were in their boat mending the nets. And immediately he called them, and they left their father Zebedee in the boat with the hired servants and followed him. (Mark 1:14–20)

Jesus arrives on the scene with a message, an attractive message. It's a message people can't get enough of. He comes "proclaiming the gospel of God," that is, the *good news* of God.

Most people in your context think that Christianity is all about advice—that it's a list of "dos and don'ts." They couldn't be more wrong.

We react far differently to news than we do to advice. Imagine a young wife who, nine months earlier, sent her husband off to war. It's been a devastating, frightening, and lonely nine months. But a good friend gives her some sound and helpful advice to help her through. The friend tells her, "Be patient. Stay busy. Find yourself a good hobby and some projects to fill your time until your husband comes home. Keep writing him those letters. Stay strong."

How is the young wife going to react? She'll likely appreciate the advice and try to absorb it. It will be a help of sorts, but the advice doesn't produce joy or relief.

Imagine, though, the same young wife in the same situation. Imagine that same friend coming over, but instead of offering *good advice* she speaks *good news*: "Did you hear the news? The war is over! Your husband is coming home! He's coming back!"

How will that young wife respond? Will she break down and cry tears of relief? Will she run into her friend's arms, screaming and celebrating? One thing is certain, she will rejoice! People react differently to hearing good news than they do when hearing good advice. Advice gives people more work to do. Good news gives people freedom.

Jesus didn't come with advice for us to absorb and follow; He came with news. The word *gospel* means "good news." It is news that brings joy. The gospel is history-making, life-shaping, paradigm-shattering news. It is news about something done in history that changes you, that changes everything, forever. Jesus does something so radical, so violent, so dramatic, and it seals this good news and makes a way for us to join the Big Story.

It is this news that makes Jesus so attractive and that separates Him from all other religions. He didn't come dispensing advice on how to clean yourself up and make yourself better. He didn't offer a list of action items or set of instructions about things you must *do* to find God, freedom, rest, or peace. No. Jesus came saying that you can be known, loved, set free, forgiven, and made new.

This new life is open to anyone. Anyone can be made new, made clean, set free, given a relationship with the living God. And it is free. There is no earning it. It is yours, no strings attached. The gospel says all this has *been done*. There isn't any more doing to do. It's not advice, so don't treat the gospel like mere advice. Jesus came, lived, died, and rose again to earn the way to God, freedom, rest, and peace for you.

Nobody else has ever spoken this way, arriving on the scene and offering *news* of a new life instead of *advice* on how to achieve a better life. Founders of other religions and worldviews ask you to do something—to perform and obey—to bring your doing to the table in order to enjoy the benefits of karma, nirvana, inner peace, a better future, salvation, or whatever the benefit might be. Christianity is the one faith whose founder tells us not to bring Him our doing, but our *need*.

The Search for a True Story

But there is more to this story. It is not enough to merely say that Jesus brings true news and good news. No, we must know His story—how His existence, arrival, teaching, and deeds fit within human history.

Jesus is part of a much larger story, an epic story. This story has all the makings of the best, truest stories—conflict, tension, and drama. It comes with that essential, "Uh-oh, how will this be resolved?" ingredient that all the best books and movies have.

When Jesus shows up in Mark 1, He says, "The time is fulfilled" (v. 15). What is fulfilled? What time? See, God has been doing something throughout all of history, through this Big Story told in the Bible, and Jesus is the apex and fulfillment of that story. All the "uh-oh" moments are resolved in Jesus Christ.

Each one of us has a story that we believe, one we use to make sense of our lives and our world. Some of us draw our stories from family legacy while others try to escape the story of their family. Some live the stories of pursuing success, fame, or wealth. Some of us want to live the story of a hero but are stuck in what seems like a boring story. Some of us fit our lives into a story taught by a religion or a philosopher or thinker we admire. Some of us attach ourselves to the dominant storyline of the city we live in, chasing pleasure in Las Vegas or power in Washington, D.C.[10] We may not even be aware of it or ever have even thought of it in those terms, but it is true. We can't live without a sense of story. The best way I know to get this across is to again share a quote from the Introduction:

> The same impulse that makes us want our books to have a plot makes us want our lives to have a plot. We need to feel that we are getting somewhere, making progress. There is something in us that is not satisfied with a merely psychological explanation of our lives. It doesn't do justice to our conviction that we are on some kind of journey or quest, that there must be some deeper meaning to our lives than whether we feel good about ourselves. Only people who have lost the sense of adventure, mystery, and romance worry about their self-esteem. And at that point what they need is not a good therapist, but a good story. Or more precisely, the central question for us should not be, "What personality dynamics explain my behavior?" but rather, "What sort of story am I in?"[11]

There is only one true story that can make sense of all we encounter in this broken and beautiful world. I call this the Big Story. It's the story of the Scriptures. I am going to lay all my cards on the table and state clearly what Jesus tells us, what the Scriptures tell us, and what I have come to believe: You cannot be free until you come under the reign of the Scriptures, until you accept and live into the Big Story. For those of you who don't believe this story, I'm not asking you to accept it right now. What I am asking is for you to consider this story, to examine it and try it on. Explore and see if this story is true. I want you to test the Big Story against whatever story you're using right now to make sense out of your life.

Your Story and Starting in the Middle

Some of the best stories are ones that don't start at the beginning. They jump in at the middle and draw us in by introducing the best characters and the most dramatic moments without revealing the beginning or the ending just yet. Jesus is the most important character in our stories. His life dramatically shapes our stories. There is no happy ending (or happy middle) without Jesus being the main character in our story, the leading man, the driving force.

And so, in one sense, this book starts in the middle of the story so that you can meet the main character and begin to know Him and trust Him. I want to give away the climax, the most important and dramatic part of this story, but this story needs a beginning, so we will go there next. Because every great story needs not only a great main character, but a strong start. Let's take the first step of our climb up the mountain, and begin Act 1.

STORY CONTRAST (JESUS VS. _____ **):** At the center of the Big Story stands Jesus, whose love both disturbs us and frees us. What, or who, stands at the center of the stories people around you believe? In what ways does having Jesus at the center of the story make for a better story?

ACTION STEP: Draw your life story. Get out a piece of paper, draw a line across the center of the page, and graph the most significant moments of your life. Aim to graph about ten significant moments, like in the example below.[12] What patterns do you notice? Who or what has most significantly shaped your story? How does your story fit within the Big Story?

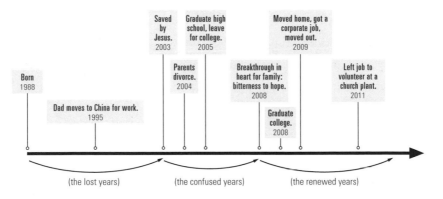

Saved by Jesus. 2003

Graduate high school, leave for college. 2005

Moved home, got a corporate job, moved out. 2009

Born 1988

Parents divorce. 2004

Breakthrough in heart for family: bitterness to hope. 2008

Left job to volunteer at a church plant. 2011

Dad moves to China for work. 1995

Graduate college. 2008

(the lost years)   (the confused years)   (the renewed years)

RECOMMENDED READING: Tim Keller, *Counterfeit Gods: The Empty Promises of Money, Sex, and Power, and the Only Hope That Matters* (Dutton, 2009). My friend Eric bought about one thousand copies of this book, and he gives copies away to everyone he can. You'd like my friend Eric, and you'd like this book.

"I had always felt life a story, and if there is a story there is a storyteller."

—G. K. Chesterton[1]

. . .

"The world does not revolve around you."

—Anonymous

. . .

2

ACT 1:

GOD

Have you ever read a book that changed your life? Sometimes it doesn't take a whole book, but just a sentence. When I was twenty years old, I asked for cash for Christmas, but instead my mom gave me a book. At first I was disappointed, but then I began reading. The book was by A. W. Tozer and was called *The Knowledge of the Holy*, and on the first page sat a sentence that changed my life.

What comes into our minds when we think about God is the most important thing about us.[2]

This is a bold claim. It makes sense. Think about it. What you think about God is the most important thing about you because it shapes everything else in your life. What you believe (or don't believe) about God drives how you live. If you think of God as a thunderbolt-throwing deity, watching everything you do and waiting for you to misbehave so He can blast you, that's going to cause you to live with quite a bit of fear and anxiety. Or if you think of God as a Santa Claus in the sky who exists to give you gifts and entertain, that's going to cause you to live as though God exists to serve your every wish and need. But if you have a true view of God, a biblical view, that will greatly affect how you live as well. A true view of God will both radically disturb your life and set you free. What comes into your mind when you think about God is the most important thing about you. It will shape your life and shape the epitaph written on your gravestone.

Gravestones

Recently while I was working on some ideas for a sermon, I walked to a cemetery about a half-mile from my house. I'm a little odd that way; when I want ideas, I take walks where people are buried. In the corner of this old cemetery, there were two gravestones that caught my attention. The first was a large marble gravestone that read:

Mrs. Susan Armes
Born 1787
And Passed to Higher Life 1875

Just a few yards away from this stone was a small, simple gravestone that had this inscription:

Little Ernest
Beloved son of J & L Rockwell
1902–1913

Do you ever think about what happened to the people buried in cemeteries? Where did they go once they quit breathing? Mrs.

Susan Armes lived eighty-eight years on this earth, and Little Ernest lived eleven years—then what? Little Ernest's gravestone says nothing about life after death, but the eighty-eight-year-old's gravestone says that she "Passed to Higher Life." Do we believe that, that there is a *higher* life on the other side of death? Every thinking person should have a list of life questions, and at the top of that list should be the question, "Does God exist, and if so, what is He like?"

Does God exist?

If so, what is He like?

We started exploring the Big Story in Chapter 1, but we didn't start at the beginning. We started with Jesus. Like many movie-makers do, we started with a key point in the plot of this story, and now we're going to go back to the beginning and see how it's all set up. I laid out the premise that all people live their lives believing some kind of story to make sense out of their life. Where I live is a lot like where you live—it's a mixture of stories. My city is a mixture of people who all believe very different stories that give very different answers to questions about life, death, and divinity. Amid this diversity, for thousands of years, men and women from all corners of the globe have discovered that the God revealed in the Bible is the one Storyteller whose storytelling rings true and satisfying. This storytelling begins with the first four words of the Bible.

Act 1: God

A book can change your life. A sentence can change your life. And sometimes just four words can change your life. The Bible begins with four powerful words that affect everything:

Genesis 1:1, "In the beginning, God . . ."

This is Act 1 of the Bible. Act 1 is about God. Every act of the Big Story is mainly about God (instead of being mainly about us), but four acts are about both God *and* us. Act 1 is unique. Act 1 is exclusively about God.

We often insist on living as if we are the beginning, the origin, the primary character. We live life under the banner of "In the beginning, me." But the Bible doesn't begin with "In the beginning, Justin," or "In the beginning, [insert your name here]." It boldly states, "In the beginning, God."

If life were about you, we couldn't call it the "Big Story." We'd have to call it the "Small Story." And that wouldn't be a very interesting story. I hope you have an interesting life. I hope that when you die, people remember you for a few years. But by and large, you're just not that interesting. You're a small, little person in a massive universe that doesn't really notice you. You need a story, and a God, that can make sense of your little life in this big universe. Actually, contrary to how most people think, the more you can see that God is big and you are small—that life is about Him, not you— the happier you'll be. But I'm getting ahead of myself here . . .

For now just get this: The start of this story isn't, "In the beginning, me." It's, "In the beginning, God."

In the beginning, God.

In the beginning, God.

In the beginning, God.

Drill that into your thinking.

The Happy God

The Bible begins with God already there. The Bible makes no attempt to explain the existence of God. There's no argument, no proofs, no evidence. There are just proclamations. Proofs of God's existence have their place, but they are kind of extracurricular and not tied to the Bible's main point. What is this main point? *In the beginning, God!* It's a bold proclamation that you must wrestle with, that you must believe or reject.

There never was a time when God was not. God has always existed. But why does God exist? Primarily, God exists for God. God loves to be God.

Imagine walking out the front door of your home and bumping into God. What would He be like? The New Testament, a portion of the Bible that we'll be talking about later, speaks of "the blessed God."[3] God is blessed, and in the Bible, *blessed* means "happy" or "joyful." This God is a happy God. He lacks nothing. He isn't deficient in any way. Comedian Joe Brown observes God and His followers this way, "I have no understanding of a long-faced Christian. If God is anything, he must be joy."[4]

God has existed forever. Think about eternity with me for a moment. When I was about six years old, an adult tried to explain to me what it meant that God is eternal, that He had no beginning and no end. I felt like my head was going to explode. Sometimes that truth of eternity still makes me feel that way. We simply don't have categories to understand *eternal*. Think about this biblical claim with me right now: In the beginning, God. God had no beginning. God began all beginning.

God has existed forever and has been happy forever. Why? Because He gets to enjoy Himself. Have you ever heard someone say that God created the world, that He created humanity, because He was lonely or bored? Don't ever listen to that nonsense. God didn't come up with Adam and Eve, the first humans, and spontaneously shout, "Oh yes, humans! Now I'm complete." No, God doesn't need us for His happiness or fulfillment.

As the story of the Bible unfolds, we learn more about God and what His existence was like before creating the universe. We learn that God has always existed in perfect community as *one* God in *three* persons: Father, Son, and Holy Spirit (people call this the Trinity, which means "three-in-one"). It's this mysterious reality that satisfies God, the fact that God is tri-personal. He isn't lonely. He isn't bored. God the Father has always lavished His love and praise on the Son. God the Son has always basked in the love of the Father and honored Him in return. God the Spirit has always been pointing attention to and praising the Father and the Son. And God the three-in-one has being doing this, in Himself, for all eternity. God loves to be God. Always has. Always will.

It's up to you whether you believe this or not. But if you don't believe in the God of the Bible, the Trinitarian, happy God, then you have to believe in something else that requires just as much (if not more) faith. Believing that there is no God, believing that this universe is ruled by multiple gods at war with each other (like many of the ancient Greeks believed), or believing that this universe is ruled by karma or some other impersonal force—these are all beliefs requiring faith. One way or another, you have faith in something.

God is God whether you believe in Him or not. His existence doesn't depend on you and His happiness doesn't depend on you. He doesn't depend on you. It's the other way around.

There are no people involved, interspersed, or included in the beginning of this story. "In the beginning, GOD . . ." Not one other person. God has been enjoying Himself for all eternity and isn't about to stop now. He is utterly independent. I don't tell you this to offend you, I tell you this to set you free.

The Pursuit of Happiness

If God doesn't need us, then why do we exist? Blaise Pascal, the seventeenth-century philosopher and mathematician, had this to say about man's existence: "All men seek happiness without exception. They all aim at this goal however different the means they use to attain it. . . . They will never make the smallest move but with this as its goal. This is the motive of all the actions of all men, even those who contemplate suicide."[5]

According to Pascal, man exists for the pursuit of happiness. Everything we do is for happiness. Even those who consider ending their lives are motivated by happiness. The pursuit of happiness is the conscious or unconscious motive that drives both our good and bad decisions.

Bruce Springsteen, the rock and roll hall of famer and unintentional theologian, says that "everybody's got a hungry heart."[6] He's so sure that he wrote a whole song about it. We are all hungry. We have an emptiness that needs to be filled. If we take the time to observe the world around us we can easily see that this is true. Everyone is trying to fill themselves with something, trying to satisfy the hunger in their heart.

Prosperity, promotions, praise, popularity, power, and people—these are the "Ps" we pursue in our hunger. We feel like if we get any or all of these Ps, our hearts will be satisfied, and we'll be okay. The hunger will go away, right?

Sadly, the answer is no. Even if we achieve the Ps, all we're doing is what I call "kissing boo-boos." Let me explain. I have three young sons, and when they get hurt we call it a "boo-boo." They scrape their knees or bump their heads and come running to me crying, "Daddy, kiss the boo-boo!" And I do. In their minds this is a magical cure. All the pain goes away, and they're fine because I kissed the boo-boo.

But this only works because they have never been seriously hurt. Sure, a kiss will make them feel better about a bump or a scratch, but kissing boo-boos doesn't work for serious pain. And the day of serious hurt comes for everyone. There comes a time when kissing our boo-boos with prosperity or power or people just won't work. We have been filling our hearts with the Ps, but someday we're going to realize they just don't satisfy. Difficult circumstances are going to come, we're going to get hurt, something big is going to happen and we're going to come to the realization that all those Ps are just kisses on boo-boos. They don't genuinely fill our hungry hearts.

That's because we hunger for something bigger. We need something massive to satisfy the deep hunger inside of us.

"Human history is the long terrible story of man trying to find something other than God which will make him happy."[7] That's how C. S. Lewis, the late English author, describes humanity's pursuit of happiness. This is why we're hungry. We have been feeding ourselves, trying to fill that emptiness with something other than God. But nothing smaller than God can fill the human heart. Nothing smaller than God can satisfy the starvation inside of us.

Imagine a friend walked up to you and offered you a $500 gift certificate to the best steakhouse in town and told you to get anything you wanted. You could order that perfect, medium-rare filet mignon, the twice-baked potato, the bottle of cabernet, and whichever appetizers and desserts suit your fancy. Now imagine responding, "No, I'm good. I've got five dollars in my wallet. I'll just head over to McDonald's for a burger and a Coke."

That's how we respond to God.

We settle for spending our last five dollars on some gristly, cheap burger on a stale bun with a slimy pickle when we could have a juicy steak dinner at the best restaurant in town. We are being offered God and we settle for a Big Mac.

Something is wrong with us. We need help. Only a fool would do what we have all done—choose McDonald's over the five-hundred-dollar feast; choose hollow pleasures over the living God.

Becoming a Christian, choosing to believe the Big Story, is simply a matter of getting serious about the pursuit of happiness. It's a matter of ditching the cheap pleasures that never satisfied in order to experience the happiness that we are designed to enjoy.

Enjoying God

Doesn't this make sense? God has always existed, always been perfectly happy, always been in perfect community, and always enjoyed perfect love. And it is out of this love that He created us. How else would we be satisfied but with Him? Of course everything else fails to satisfy.

Our third son is named Augustine (we call him Gus). We named him after St. Augustine, the fourth-century theologian and pastor who was a giant in his day and remains one still for his defense of the true God in the face of attacks and skepticism. St. Augustine lived a reckless and unsatisfying life throughout his youth until God got ahold of him and transformed his whole life. He went on to write a book that is still an enormously respected work today, 1700 years later, called *Confessions*. In this book he says, "God, you made us for yourself and our hearts are restless until they find their rest in you."[8]

God exists for God and we exist for God. Our existence doesn't make sense apart from God.

I love what a man named David says in Psalm 16, a poetic part of the Bible. "You make known to me the path of life; in your presence there is fullness of joy; at your right hand are pleasures forevermore" (v. 11). Do we think about God that way? At His right hand are pleasures forever! In His presence is *fullness* of joy! David tried all the Ps (prosperity, promotions, praise, popularity, power, people) and found that they left him hungry and empty; they didn't deliver their promises. Only in God did he find true pleasure and rest. Imagine that—finding rest and satisfaction in God instead of in the smaller things God created.

Ever since God made us in His image, we have been returning the favor. We've been making every attempt to re-create God in our image. We have been operating with false ideas of who God is and what He's like. We need to return to Scripture, what God says about Himself, to get a true picture of what He is really like.

I'm in love with my wife. I'm in love with her for many reasons, but a big reason for my love is because I know her attributes. I know that she is fun, humble, smart, selfless, and happy. And these attributes inspire me to better enjoy and love her.

It's not so different with God. He has attributes that we need to know if we are to be moved to love Him, trust Him, and walk with Him. God has numerous attributes. He is infinite, holy, just, unchanging, all-knowing . . . I could go on and on. There have been volumes written on God's attributes.[9] There are three attributes of

God, though, that are especially important to understand because all the others fall under them. They are the three suitcases into which all His other attributes can be packed. They are the three legs on which the stool stands. These are the three most important things you could know about God.

God Is SOVEREIGN

When I was twenty years old I took a road trip across the country with my best friend. While driving through Colorado, we "randomly" bumped into my pastor from Santa Barbara, Reed Jolley, who was vacationing with his family. I saw him and said something like "No way! This is crazy; it's so random." Almost immediately, Reed gently corrected me. He said a sentence that changed my perspective on life: "If you believe in a single accident, you might as well be an atheist."

If there is a single circumstance that can occur outside of God's control, then God is not God, and He cannot be trusted. That's what sovereignty means—God is God, no one else is, and He has absolute control.

A pine cone cannot fall from a tree unless God is involved. A bumblebee cannot pollenate a flower or sting your arm apart from the will of God. Money cannot enter or exit your bank account apart from the sovereignty of God. Little Ernest cannot be born or be buried in that grave just a half-mile from my house apart from God's will. Legislation cannot be passed in this country or in any other apart from God's sovereignty. You hold this book in your hands because God sovereignly allows you to hold this book in your hands. Everything is under His sovereign rule.

Some of us believe that God is a bit like the president. He has a lot of power and authority, but there are checks and balances to limit Him. He is limited by our human choices, the events of the future, the wrongs of the past, or by those who do not believe in Him. Some of His legislations could be vetoed. His popularity can ebb and flow. But God is not like that at all. There are no limits to His rule and power.

The writer of Psalm 135 says it like this in verses 5 and 6, "For I know that the Lord is great, and that our Lord is above all gods. *Whatever the Lord pleases, he does*, in heaven and on earth, in the seas and all deeps." God does what He pleases whenever He wants and in whatever place He wants!

A few months ago, in the space of a single afternoon, this reality was crystalized for me. In the space of five minutes, I received two difficult emails, one from my landlord and the other regarding the space our church was renting. The first email made it clear that there was a very real possibility I might have to immediately up and move my family out of the home we were living in, a home we were just beginning to love and settle into. The second threatened our church's ability to continue meeting in the location where we were renting space for our Sunday gatherings. In five minutes, the well-being of both my family and my flock had been threatened. My heart began to race and worry swept over me.

But God is sovereign. Amid the growing worry, somehow I reminded myself of this fact and I said to God, "God, these guys threatened Your house and Your church. What are you going to do about it?" The home I rent isn't mine, and it isn't the landlord's. The church I lead isn't mine, the congregation's, or the building owner's. Ultimately, it all belongs to God. I could trust God in that situation, and you can trust Him in those threatening, frightening, or difficult situations you face. I remember the days when I used to think I was in control of my life. I'm glad those days are over. There's nothing quite like the feeling of being able to completely trust someone else with every detail of your life.

And it is not just these domestic, relatively small fears in which God can be trusted. Throughout history, Christians have trusted God with their very lives. Corrie ten Boom had enough faith to hide Jews in her Amsterdam home during the Nazi occupation because she knew it was right, even though, should she have been found out, it could have cost her life. Brother Andrew spent decades sneaking Bibles and Christian literature behind the Iron Curtain into Eastern Europe and the former USSR, even though it could have cost him prison or death. House churches across China have continued to meet for decades even as their pastors have been jailed and tortured.

All these believers knew one thing and held fast to it, even as fear and pain surrounded and threatened to overcome them. God owns us. He owns everything. He is sovereign over all things. He can be trusted.

God Is WISE

God governs the galaxies and your problems and your pain and your prayers. He sees it all. But if God is sovereign, and not also wise, you can't truly trust Him. Why would anyone want to trust a being who is absolutely powerful but rather stupid and lacking in good judgment? That's a recipe for disaster.

But God manages the universe in absolute wisdom. He sees everything in perfect perspective. God is never confused, never has been confused, and never will be confused. God is never worried nor will He ever be. God never makes a mistake.

Many of us, though, live as if God is dumb. We think God needs our help or our input to gain a better understanding of our situation and to really grasp what's going on. But God has perfect perspective. And He doesn't just see more, He sees all. God misses nothing and knows exactly what everything means in relation to everything else.

And God has a plan. Whether or not we see it or feel it, it is there. It's there because God is God, and He is perfectly wise.

My son Hudson is a crazy man. He's four years old at the time I'm writing this. If my wife and I don't keep an eye on this kid, he's gone; he just runs away. We walk into a store and two seconds later we look around, and Hudson is gone. He'll dash into the street. He'll sprint into big crowds and disappear. He could get himself into crazy, dangerous situations. But we stop him.

My wife and I know more than Hudson knows. We see more than he sees. We see the oncoming car or the creepy-looking person hovering nearby. We know the risks and the potential dangers, and Hudson doesn't. And this is how God is with us.

There are things you want to be doing right now, some circumstances you want in your life. You are ready to dash out and make it happen, to grab hold of those things you want. But God might not be letting you. God sees the oncoming car and the creepy person hovering nearby. He knows the danger you might be putting yourself in, and you don't. God watches over you with perfect wisdom and absolute sovereignty.

But God is not merely sovereign and wise.

God Is GOOD

People who are truly powerful and truly wise, but fail to be good, are terrifying beings. If there is a God who is sovereign over all things and knows all things, but who is not also good, then that God is to be feared above all other beings because He is capable of unspeakable terrors. But if God is sovereign over all things, perfectly wise, and *perfectly good*, then He is to be trusted above all other beings.

See, God's goodness is not a mood. All of us get in good moods sometimes and bad moods other times. Some of you grew up with abusive or alcoholic fathers. You never knew what his mood would be, and there was no telling what would trigger a change. Many of us view God a bit like that: the God who strikes with thunderbolts. What is He thinking right now? Am I about to set Him off and get roasted? But God doesn't have moods. He is always good.

God's goodness never takes a break. However good you think God is, He's better than that. God is better than the best you think He could be. And so you can trust Him. This is hard for us to fathom because we know no sinless people. Every relationship we have ever had has been with a sinner, an imperfect person, but God has no sin. He will never fail us.

Another view of God that people have is that of the Santa Claus God. This version of God gives all we ask for and never denies a request, so long as we're practicing fairly "nice" behavior. But there will come a time when reality hits: you ask God for something and do not get it. What then? You won't believe in Him anymore because your very notion of God has been destroyed. But believing in this idea of God isn't freedom at all; it's captivity.

God calls us to believe in Him at all times, to trust in His goodness at all times. If we can believe that God is God and we are not, *that* is freedom. It is foundational Christianity. It is the basic message of the Bible. God is God and you are not. So you can be yourself and rest because God is busy being Himself—ruling your life and the universe with His perfect sovereignty, wisdom, and goodness. God's job is to be God. Your job: let God be God.

My friend Ed is from England. Thus, everything he says sounds smart. He and his family have been in some difficult circumstances and he recently left me a voicemail. In his extra-smart English accent Ed said to me, "But the Lord is our shepherd and He will care for us." And that has been ringing in my mind and heart ever since.

Whatever you're facing, imagine Ed, English accent and all, saying to you, "But the Lord is your shepherd and He will care for you." You might not believe any of this yet, but I bet you at least want to believe it. God is sovereign. God is wise. God is *good*. And you can always trust Him. Other stories don't offer you this.[10]

Judge or Father?

The Bible is about God. The story of the Bible is about God. It is not about us working our way up to God. It's about Him working His way down to us, to our broken world, in order to fix us and free us.

In a later chapter, we're going to explore questions of pain: why is it here and where did it come from? What the Bible is clear about, though, is that pain exists because of us, because of our sin—our rebellion against God. And the root of all our sin is that we have failed to live in line with Genesis 1:1. We haven't lived,

"In the beginning, God." We've lived, "In the beginning, me." We have sought to be god of our own lives. My friend Bernard Bell puts it this way:

> We too easily give our devotion to that which has not created us. But more subtly, we align God to our programs rather than aligning ourselves to God's program. This is what happens when our thinking begins with self not with God. . . . We fail to start with the first verse of the Bible: "In the beginning, God." . . . If your thinking does not rest on God but on yourself, if you forget "In the beginning, God," if you have too small a view of God or too high a view of self, then you are placing too great a burden on yourself, a burden you were not made to carry.[11]

See, we get life backward. We start with ourselves, not with God.

Everybody on the planet already has a relationship with God. The question is this: Is God our Judge or is He our Father? The Bible tells the story about how this God, as our Judge, sends someone (Jesus) to pay our judgment price, to be punished for our sins, so that we are free to know God as Father.

Many of us, as we consider this relationship with God, go back time and again to events and circumstances that we think prevent us from being close to Him as a Father. We think on our own mistakes and sins, the things others have done to us, the lies we have told or the ones we have believed. But God is bigger than all those things, even the pile of them we have in our lives.

God is bigger than your dreams, even the broken ones. He is bigger than all your fears, all your shame, all your scars, all your regrets. He is bigger than your enemies, your weaknesses, or your handicaps. God is bigger than you.

It is so easy to think wrongly about God, that many of us have become accustomed to it. We have failed to have a true biblical picture of God in our minds and hearts. We see how humans behave and operate—full of weakness and failure and hypocrisy—and it is natural to assume God must be like that.

But the true God is never wrong, never gets tired, is never bound, and can always do what He wants (and what He wants is always right). He is never moody, never worries, and never runs out of resources. The true God never compromises who He truly is. He is never unfaithful, never lies, and never, ever leaves. He never changes. And He always keeps His promises.

This God is perfectly sovereign, perfectly wise, and perfectly good. He is One on whom you can bank your life. He is a perfect Father to all those who trust Him. Instead of condemning you, He can adopt you into His family.

This God exists to be praised, enjoyed, loved, trusted, and honored. And so we should run to Him, cling to Him, and give every bit of ourselves to Him. He is calling us to Himself for His glory.

Like the old Sunday school song goes: "He's got the whole world in His hands." He's got your hopes and dreams, He's got you and me, He's got your future, He's got the whole world in those sovereign, wise, and *good* hands.

You already have a relationship with this God. God is the author of your life, the author of your story. The question is whether you relate to God as your Judge (because you are still insisting on being the god of your own life) or whether you relate to God as your Father (because you're letting God be God—ruling, leading, and forgiving—and you're letting you be you, a forgiven and loved son or daughter of God).

God is not a character in your story. You are a character in His story.

STORY CONTRAST (GOD VS._____): The Big Story begins with God. What, or who, stands at the beginning of the stories people believe in your context? In what ways does having God at the beginning of the story make for a better story?

ACTION STEP: Memorize and meditate on two sentences:
   (1) "In the beginning, God."
   (2) God is sovereign, wise, and good.

Many of the problems you face in life can be navigated well by simply knowing and living in line with these massive truths. These are foundational pillars of the Big Story.

RECOMMENDED READING: *The Jesus Storybook Bible* by Sally Lloyd-Jones (Zondervan, 2007). This isn't just a book for kids; almost every week I recommend this book to adults, to people who don't yet believe in the Big Story and people who've believed this story for decades.

"The world now consumes films, novels, theatre, and television in such quantities and with such ravenous hunger that the story arts have become humanity's prime source of inspiration, as it seeks to order chaos and gain insight into life. Our appetite for story is a reflection of the profound human need to grasp patterns of living. . . . Story isn't a flight from reality but a vehicle that carries us on our search for reality, our best effort to make sense out of the anarchy of existence."

—Robert McKee[1]

• • •

"Story has unquestionably become the dominant means of understanding our world, ourselves, and each other. When neighbors and strangers meet today, they often ask not, 'What do you do?' but 'What is your story?'" —

Leslie Leyland Fields[2]

• • •

"You were made for God, not vice versa, and life is about letting God use you for his purposes, not your using him for your own purpose."

—Rick Warren[3]

• • •

3

ACT 2:

CREATION

Last year I traveled to Arkansas for a leadership retreat with other church leaders from across the country. On the first night, ten of us men gathered in a large living room and were asked to share a defining story from our lives that had deeply shaped the men we are today. The strongest, most intimidating man in the room began to share his story. This pastor—a former college football player, nearly three hundred pounds and brandishing biceps the size of my waist—began to captivate us with his detailed storytelling. He was composed, articulate, and enthusiastic as he shared this story from his life. Then a turning point came.

His voice changed and cracked. He began to shake. He began describing a pivotal afternoon in his teenage years when his dad, a man whose respect he desired more than anything in the world, evaluated his report card and called him "stupid." As he told us this, tears began flowing down his cheeks and kept coming. He shook and he cried, reliving the event twenty years later, telling us how he still hears that stinging voice of his father in his head: "Stupid!" He'd tried to shake it his whole life, but ever since hearing those words from his dad, this massive man had thought of himself as stupid.

Identity

Identity drives everything in life. Everything you do, every decision you make, is driven by your identity. It is driven by how you see yourself.

Where do you get your identity? What voices are in your head that tell you who you are? What stories are you believing that are shaping how you see yourself?

Different cities with different cultures tell us different things about identity. In New York people ask, "Where do you live?" That's the defining question. Is it a wealthy neighborhood, poor neighborhood, hipster hood, intellectual elitist hood, the Bronx, or Manhattan? You are where you're from.

In Washington, D.C., it's, "Who do you know?" It's power politics. Are you an insider? Do you know the right people? If not, you're not worth knowing.

In Silicon Valley, where I live, it's, "What do you do?" Your identity is tied to your career and your success or lack of success in that career.

And other places ask different questions to define us. "Where did you go to school?" "What family are you from?" In highly religious environments, you even find the question, "Where do you go to church?"

Sometimes we even go on a search of our identity because we realize that where we're from, who we know, or what we do is too shallow and hollow to truly define us. A couple years ago, I went digging to learn more about where I came from. I started researching my background and genealogy.

The name Buzzard is a bit weird. It turns out I have Swiss roots. In 1735, Balthazar Bossart, with his wife and three sons, left Switzerland to come to the United States (although it wasn't even the United States yet, since this was forty years prior to the signing of the Declaration of Independence). His name, Bossart, was changed to Buzzard when he got here.

When I learned about my Swiss roots, I thought it all added up and made more sense out of who I am and what I love. I love mountains because it's in my blood; my people are from the Alps! I thought this must be why I love chocolate and fondue so much. It's why I love knives, chiefly Swiss Army knives. My "Swissness" made sense of me. (I'm being funny, but you can see how a search for identity and connection to our roots can help us make sense of ourselves.)

We all have these battles of conflicted thoughts about our identities. But the search must go deeper than words spoken to us in our adolescence and the actions of our ancestors. We must go back to the beginning.

The Beginning

Maybe if we go all the way back to the beginning, to *our* beginning, to the creation of the world, maybe there will be something there. Maybe that story will have something to say to us about who we are. Maybe it will tell us the true story of our identity.

Act 1 involved God only. In Act 2, God remains the main character, but now humans show up—we have a critical role to play in this Big Story.

> In the beginning, God created the heavens and the earth. The earth was without form and void, and darkness was over the face of the deep. And the Spirit of God was hovering over the face of the waters. And God said, "Let there be light," and there was light. And God saw that the light was good. And God separated the light from the darkness. God called the light Day, and the darkness he called Night. And there was evening and there was morning, the first day. (Genesis 1:1–5)

God created out of nothing. There was no pantry of ingredients. No "A dash of this for stars and a pinch of that for animals." He created out of complete nothingness because He's God and He alone could do so.

He created with His voice. With only His voice. He simply spoke and the universe came into existence. What we imagine as mere sounds had the power to create everything out of nothing when exhaled by God.

How many times have we tried to do this same thing? I pull into a restaurant parking lot on a busy Friday night and out of my mouth come the words, "Let there be a parking space." We suffer from verbal impotence. But God's sentences create solar systems.

Big Claims

I realize there are claims wrapped in these statements that need to be wrestled with. The Bible begins with the reality of God's existence but makes no effort to prove it. God's story begins not with proofs but with proclamation. God is there. He is the one true God. He created the universe.

A person must think through these claims. They are big and bold and affect everything. If we believe these claims about God, they shape our stories. They are so big that they shape our stories even if we don't believe these claims. And if these claims are in fact true, then the voice of God is the voice to which we must listen.

There's a sentence in the Bible that reads, "The fool says in his heart, 'There is no God.'"[4] You have two stories to choose from: either "In the beginning, God" or "There is no God." To believe there is no God requires a sort of dire consistency exemplified by the twentieth-century philosopher Bertrand Russell when he said, "Man is the product of causes which had no pre-vision of the end they were achieving . . . his origin, his growth, his hopes and fears, his loves and his beliefs, are but the outcome of accidental collocations of atoms."[5] To say there is no God is to remove any meaningful purpose from your life, to make your story one of chaos, happenstance, and accidents. Your hopes, dreams, fears, and joys all add up to a grand nothing. If you believe there is no God, you don't have a Big Story. You have a very short and discouraging story. As Thomas Dubay states, "For the thoughtful atheist, death must loom as a crushing catastrophe. Everything good, noble, beautiful experienced throughout life is about to vanish, not simply for a week or two, not only for a century, but forever. On the atheist's premise death is a nightmare unbroken by a dawn."[6]

The Talking God

The God of the universe is a talker. One of the first things we learn about God in the Bible is that He is a speaker, a communicator.

And His voice is one worth listening to.

One man, Moses, listened closely to the voice of God. Moses was the writer of Genesis, this first book of the Bible that we're looking at right now. Moses wrote Genesis as the people of God (also known as Israel) made the trek from Egypt to the Promised Land over the course of several decades. This was not just a nomadic wandering or minor road trip; it was a truly treacherous and defining passage from slavery to freedom.

The journey led Israel through the lands of numerous enemy nations—Egyptians, Amorites, Babylonians, Canaanites—with strong armies and a thirst for war. Not only were these nations frightening for their military strength, they had totally different and diametrically opposed beliefs and worldviews about why the world existed and who created it.

The Babylonians believed a story of creation called the *Enuma Elish*. It told the tale of a universe with many gods constantly warring with each other—violent and unpredictable gods. This story explains that the world was created out of this conflict. Two gods, Marduk (the storm god) and Tiamat (the goddess of water), battled each other, and Marduk killed Tiamat. As the story goes, Marduk took Tiamat's body, hacked it in half, and used the two halves to create the matter of the universe.[7]

So it is in the shadow of these frightening nations and fearfully defining stories that we must hear the story of Genesis. It was shared with Israel as they battled to protect their nation physically and spiritually.

And God doesn't start off softly in His communication. He doesn't soft toss His story or play nice. No, God starts off with a dis, actually a whole series of them. You know what a dis is, short for "disrespect." It's an insult meant to disparage. And that's how God makes Himself known to Israel. As each day of creation is chronicled in Genesis, God thumbs His nose at every one of those false, foreign gods.

On day one, God disses the gods of light and darkness. "Light? You think light is a god to be worshiped? I *created* light. With a word."

On the second day, He disses the gods of sky and sea. "I created the seas. All those mighty, rolling seas you see? I made them out of nothing with My voice."

And so He goes through each day. Day three, He cuts down the gods of earth and vegetation. On day four, He slays the gods of fish and birds. On days five and six, He does away with any association people had between animals or humans and the divine; He makes absolutely clear that there is nothing to be worshiped in the mammal world.

Genesis is a powerful book. As Israel sat under the open sky and looked up at the stars that the surrounding nations worshiped, their God passed on to them the story of where those stars came from. As they passed through burning deserts and between rocky crags, they heard the story of how all this natural power and wonder was created by the words of the true God.

They learned that this good, sovereign, and wise God held their destiny in His hands. They may have been surrounded by mighty armies and enemies, but these foreign powers held no power over them. And just like Israel, our destiny is in God's hands.

God didn't tell us all this about Himself just for the sake of *explanation*, though. He told it to us for *exultation*. Life is not about simply knowing truths, it's about being wowed by what ought to wow us and worshiping what we ought to worship. Only hearts filled with the exultation of God's story will be able to handle the difficulties and disappointments that come with this life.

An exulting response to God's story looks very much like a person's response to seeing Yosemite. The first time I saw Yosemite, I was thirteen years old. As my family and I drove around a bend, we caught sight of Yosemite Valley and El Capitan and Yosemite Falls and Half Dome. I was lost in wonder. I jumped out of the minivan and started shouting and taking pictures; I was simply overwhelmed by the majesty of it all. That's exultation, and that's what our relationship with God should look like. We don't go to Yosemite and stay in the van while taking pictures of ourselves. No, we get out and get captured by the bigness and beauty. In the same way, neither should our response to God center on ourselves but rather it should be one of captured hearts and pure awe.

God created some amazing stuff. There are creatures at the bottom of the sea that humans, for all of our scientific exploration, have yet to discover. He made redwood forests and rainforests. He made the reclusive snow leopard. He made terrifying great white sharks. He made flitting hummingbirds that are less than three inches long, can flutter their wings seventy-eight times per second, and can fly nonstop all the way across the Gulf of Mexico. All this variation was God's idea, and He said it was good.

God made the planet Earth. That's big. But God made a ball of fire called the Sun that is so big it could hold one million Earths. Recently though, astronomers have discovered new planets orbiting stars far larger than our Sun.[8] They are part of completely different solar systems and galaxies. The Whirlpool galaxy is thirty-one million light years away, and it's estimated that new stars are formed there every second.

God's voice did this.

He's Talking About You

What if this voice, the one that can silence false gods and create the universe in a single breath, had something to say about who *you* are?

Throughout the creation story, God keeps giving a verdict. On the first five days, God calls His creation "good." But only one thing leads God to use the words "very good," the one thing He created in His likeness. It's the crown jewel of creation and the culmination of His handiwork.

> Then God said, "Let us make man in our image, after our likeness. And let them have dominion over the fish of the sea and over the birds of the heavens and over the livestock and over all the earth and over every creeping thing that creeps on the earth."
>
> So God created man in his own image,
> in the image of God he created him;
> male and female he created them.
>
> And God blessed them. And God said to them, "Be fruitful and multiply and fill the earth and subdue it, and have dominion over the fish of the sea and over the birds of the heavens and over every living thing that moves on the earth." And God said, "Behold, I have given you every plant yielding seed that is on the face of all the earth, and every tree with seed in its fruit. You shall have them for food. And to every beast of the earth and to every bird of the heavens and to everything that creeps on the earth, everything that has the breath of life,

I have given every green plant for food." And it was so. And God saw everything that he had made, and behold, it was *very good*. And there was evening and there was morning, the sixth day. (Genesis 1:26–31)

Of all the religions and belief systems and narratives in the world, only Christianity says you were made in the image and likeness of God. Are you reading this near someone else? Then you are reading this near the image of God. The people you can see right now, they are all people created in the image and likeness of God. I wonder if they know that? The only way they could know this is if they come into contact with this Big Story. No other story makes such a radical and beautiful claim.

What does it mean to be the image of God? One word that explains it well is "representative." As images of God, we represent God on earth. We bear His image because there is something of Him in us. We are to represent God on earth, men and women created equal, to bear God's image and represent Him. It's an identity and a calling: you are a valuable person created personally by God in His image and likeness, and your job on this planet is to creatively represent God—show forth something of God—through your life story.

But if this is true of us, why are our identities so unstable?

Lies

Were we created to live endlessly insecure lives rising and falling based on what people think about us or based on how we perform or fail to perform? Is that how God designed us?

On my flight home from that leadership retreat in Arkansas, I had a layover in Las Vegas. As soon as that Thursday afternoon flight took off from Little Rock, that plane turned into one big party. It was Vegas with wings. The scene is a little hard to describe. NASCAR-loving Arkansas rednecks launching a three-day weekend Vegas party a few hours before landing in Vegas, ordering drink after drink and letting out yells and shouts with an Arkansan drawl. I was the only Californian on the plane, not quite knowing what to do during my first in-flight Vegas party with NASCAR people.

So I decided to open my laptop and try to get my sermon ready for the next Sunday.

Somewhere between her third and fourth beer, the woman sitting next to me took notice of what I was doing, and we began talking. She opened up to me about her fourteen-year-old son, and as she shared she began to cry. Her son, she told me, was profoundly depressed. They had been to psychiatrists, doctors, and counselors, and yet he was still doing horribly. She was heartbroken and helpless.

But it was what this young man told the doctors and counselors that was so striking. He told them that he hears voices, and these voices tell him only a single word over and over again: *worthless*. Anyone would be depressed. Being fourteen is hard enough with pimples and puberty going on, but to be fourteen, navigating the recent divorce of your parents, and have a mysterious voice in your head constantly telling you you're worthless? That would damage your very identity.

What voices are in your head? It's likely not an audible voice. Maybe it's a memory of a voice from a time past. Maybe it's a cultural voice you hear from the TV or magazine racks. Many of us have been lied to. We have had voices speak into our lives telling us who we are and have latched on to those because we don't know what else to do. And by latching on we have allowed them to define how we see ourselves.

The Bible talks about the existence of a being called Satan (we'll talk about him more in the next chapter), a being who is also called "a liar and the father of lies" (John 8:44), and who is out to destroy anything God is doing here on earth, anything God calls "good." Satan authors those lies you hear.

Some have believed the professional lie that says you are what you do and how you do it. Your performance defines your worth, and so you work to succeed at the expense of all else. Some have bought into the lie of image, that how you are perceived (whether or not it's real) defines your worth. And so you use your resources and your time to create an image of . . . whatever it is you want to be known as. And there are many more lies we believe in our effort to find rest in a stable identity.

But that search for rest will never end. It will take you all the way to your grave.

Very Good

But God has already told you the truth about you. From the very beginning of creation, He has defined you with two words.

Very good.

Some of you have been searching your whole life for someone who will say that to you—a parent, a boss, a girlfriend, a spouse. If you don't find your identity in what God says, in His words, you'll be forced to build it on what other people say about you—you'll try to prove that you're "very good." And that is a foundation that will fail you. An identity that is built upon our performance rather than on God's words is an unstable identity. This is because our performance is always ebbing and flowing. Every other belief system makes you earn your identity through your performance. Only the Big Story gives you an identity before performance.

Maybe in the best marriages, families, or churches, you can hope to experience a little bit of unconditional love, but even that will be a fleeting glimpse at best. There is no love to compare to the truly unconditional love of God, and if you don't get love from Him, you will try to get it from a cheap substitute.

Imagine two men coming to propose to a woman at the same time. The first man is a faithful, loving, solid man who will care for the woman with fidelity and integrity. And as a bonus, he's handsome. The woman finds joy in just being around him; her heart skips a beat when she sees him. She knows he treasures her.

The second fellow is a different story. He has already been unfaithful, and the woman knows that it's not an anomaly but a pattern. He has abused her and treated her like garbage. He insults her, degrades her, and makes her feel small and meaningless. He frightens her and she loathes the way he makes her feel. He too is proposing. Which will she choose?

The choice seems obvious, right?

So many of us, when faced with the same sort of decision, choose the unfaithful one. We choose to build our identity on those things that hurt us and make us feel small and leave us dissatisfied.

Something has gone horribly wrong. We've chosen to run away from God. We haven't sat under this verdict He has spoken over us of "very good." Instead of resting there and flourishing, we have run from His voice. We have sought to find a verdict elsewhere from false judges.

But there is no power and no person in this world greater than God's voice—not the greatest leaders, the strongest army, the wisest counselor, the savviest entrepreneur, or the most stylish celebrity.

I think my favorite part of the Bible is Psalms, a long, poetic section of the Bible. One of my favorite psalms is Psalm 139, a poem in which a man reflects on how God made him. Listen to what Psalm 139 says about who you are:

> For you formed my inward parts;
> you knitted me together in my mother's womb.
> I praise you, for I am fearfully and wonderfully made.
> Wonderful are your works;
> my soul knows it very well.
> My frame was not hidden from you,
> when I was being made in secret,
> intricately woven in the depths of the earth.
> Your eyes saw my unformed substance;
> in your book were written, every one of them,
> the days that were formed for me,
> when as yet there were none of them. (Psalm 139:13–16)

This is the truth about you. This is your identity. Can you trust God for who you are, for how He made you? How you look, how you're wired, the family you came from (or the family you didn't have), the days He ordered for you, the life He gave you?

You are one of a kind, not an accident or "collocations of atoms," as atheist Bertrand Russell proclaims.[9] Even if your parents didn't plan you, God planned you. God *knitted* you together in your mother's womb, every physical, mental, and emotional bit of you.

Long before you ever thought about God, God was thinking about you. James Hufstetler says it like this:

> You are the result of the attentive, careful, thoughtful, intimate, detailed, creative work of God. Your personality, your sex, your height, your features, are what they are because God made them precisely that way. He made you the way he did because that is the way he wants you to be. . . . If God had wanted you to be basically and creatively different he would have made you differently. Your genes and chromosomes and creaturely distinctions—even the shape of your nose and ears—are what they are by God's design. . . . You will never really enjoy other people, you will never have stable emotions, you will never lead a life of godly contentment, you will never conquer jealousy and love others as you should until you thank God for making you the way he did.[10]

If you have an issue with who you are, then you have an issue with God. God made you precisely how He wanted you to be. We need to quit the comparing. Comparison is dangerous and goes against God's plan. It promotes sameness and flies in the face of uniqueness. But God loves uniqueness. He designed billions of unique people to each uniquely image Him here on earth. Comparison is an effort to take God's purposes and turn them upside down.

The only being who thinks more about you than you, is God. And when He thinks of you, He thinks, *very good*. He has thought that since the beginning because that's how He created you and every person before you. His story, His Word, says so. And there is nothing so true and powerful as God's Word.

Your heavenly Father speaks these words over you. And it is for the sake of these words that He sent His Son, Jesus, to unravel this identity crisis, to take what is broken and make it right again, like it was in the very beginning of the story.

See, we've lost these words. Look at the people around you. Their heads aren't buzzing with the loving voice of God singing the words, "very good." No, most people live their days hearing different voices: *stupid, worthless, not good enough*, etc. Something has gone horribly wrong. What started off so wonderfully, when God created the world and declared the first humans *very good*, has shattered to pieces. We're living the pieces. We know things used to be better than this.

What happened? What caused us to grow deaf, unable to hear that voice that tells us we are very good?

STORY CONTRAST (CREATION VS._____): After God, the beginning of the Big Story is creation. God created the universe and you with a loving purpose. Instead of creation, what stands at the beginning of the stories believed by people around you? In what ways does having creation at the beginning of the story make for a better explanation of this life?

ACTION STEP: Preach to yourself the words "very good" as often as possible. Remind yourself that this is how the Big Story starts: God looks out over the first humans, before they've done any ounce of work to prove themselves, and graciously declares them "very good." Through the restoring work of Jesus, this can be your identity (we'll discuss this more in Chapter 4). *Very good.* Declare those words to yourself morning, noon, and night.

RECOMMENDED READING: *The Walk: Steps for New and Renewed Followers of Jesus* by Stephen Smallman (P&R Publishing, 2009). I've asked every person in my church to master this book and to read it with people who are curious about Jesus and the Big Story.

"The information glut is hardly the apocalypse that some imagined might come about at the millennium. The world's not ending, it's just becoming incomprehensible."

—Joel Achenbach[1]

. . .

"No philosophy that cannot make sense of death can make sense of life either."

—Dag Hammarskjold[2]

. . .

"We're all mixed bags."

—Gordon Gekko[3]

. . .

4

ACT 3:

REBELLION

Not long ago I had the chance to do something I don't often get to do: I watched a scary movie. My wife doesn't like scary movies, but she was away with our kids. So I settled in on the couch and started my movie.

As often happens when watching such films, for some reason our outside porch light began to flicker, and the wood floors of our home began to creak (I swear this really happened). All that was missing was the lightning and thunder. As the drama of the movie unfolded and the creepy sounds continued, I became more and more freaked out—I even jumped up off the couch a few times. But I kept watching the movie because I had to know how the story would end. I was afraid, but I just had to know how the story would come to resolution. Would the main character live or die? I needed to know.

Stories are powerful things. Even a poorly directed movie or poorly written book can compel us to finish it because we need to know the ending of the story. We are wired for story.

Throughout these pages, we have come to the reality that every person on the planet believes some sort of story to help them make sense of life, the world, and how it all works. Whatever story we believe, though, needs to account for all the pain in this world. There is pain inside of us and all around us. It's everywhere. And we need to be able to make sense of it.

Poet Carl Sandburg put it like this, "Life is like an onion: you peel it off one layer at a time, and sometimes you weep."[4] Look under the layers of every life, and you will find pain. Every human has this in common. We've all felt the pain.

Just weeks after our church (Garden City Church) started in the fall of 2011, Shareef Allman went on a shooting spree in Silicon Valley. It was not far from where our church gathers on Sunday. He walked into his workplace and shot three of his coworkers to death and wounded seven others. It led to the biggest manhunt in Silicon Valley history. The next day he died in a shoot-out with authorities. Steve Jobs, the iconic cofounder and CEO of Apple, died of pancreatic cancer the same day that Shareef shot those ten people.[5]

In a single day we see two examples of the pain life brings—bullets and cancer. No doubt your life has intersected with other diseases, disabilities, dashed hopes, and funerals.

As I write this, my mom has just been diagnosed with cancer for the second time. Thirteen years ago, she was diagnosed with advanced breast cancer. She recovered, though plenty of pain was involved.[6] We thought it was over. But the cancer is back. This time my fifty-nine-year-old mom has stage IV cancer. Unless something else happens to her, this cancer will kill her. She could have a few months left. She could have a few years. We don't know. All I know is that this is painful, and I don't want my mom to die. Earlier today, I was crying my eyes out thinking about all of this. All this pain, whatever our story, we must find a story that's big enough to interpret it.

Life in this imperfect world can be so hard. I'm writing this paragraph four days after the Newtown, Connecticut, massacre, where a gunman murdered twenty-six innocent people at Sandy Hook Elementary School. Twenty of the victims were children, all first graders, who never got to open up their lunchboxes that day because their lives were abruptly extinguished. It's beyond sickening. It's evil. This is not the way things are supposed to be! Stephen Delgiadice's eight-year-old daughter barely escaped the bullets at Sandy Hook. After the shooting, Delgiadice said, "It's alarming, especially in Newtown, Connecticut, which we always thought was the safest place in America."[7] Even what we think are the safest places are vulnerable to pain, bullets, and unthinkable suffering. We need a story big enough to handle this pain.[8]

Christians Can Be the Worst

Often times Christians are the worst at talking about pain or dealing with its realities. Many Christians simply pretend there is no pain in this world. Have you ever walked into a Christian bookstore? We have only one Christian bookstore in the 8-million-person San Francisco Bay Area. Recently I visited our solitary Christian bookstore, and within its walls there is little evidence of pain, of reality. It's full of rainbows and chubby cherubs and Precious Moments figurines and pastel ceramic mugs with slogans like "Praise the Lord!" or "Hope, Happiness, and the Holy Spirit—Get Your Vitamin H Today." The art on the walls doesn't have a single dark color—everything is bright and Thomas Kinkade-ish, as though night never happens. There is little to no evidence that this world hurts.

It's almost as if many Christians believe, "God is good, so my pain and your pain aren't actually real." Most of us are very bad at facing and processing our pain. But anyone who lives long enough will experience enormous amounts of pain, and we have to ask, what do we do with all this?

Should we push it down and suppress it?

Do we ignore it completely and try to just press on?

Do we wallow in it?

Can it be fixed? Is there a solution to all this pain?

Twenty-five-year-old Jessica Perez states well the problem of pain. Abandoned by her father at age eleven and now deeply depressed, addicted to cutting herself, and anorexic to the point that she weighs barely fifty-five pounds, Jessica is trying to make sense of the pain: "I'm very lost. I feel so helpless. . . . I've always tried to be a good person. I feel like I would not have suffered the way I have without some kind of purpose behind it. If God doesn't have a purpose for this, then this universe sucks."[9]

Jessica is right. This world is full of pain. And if God doesn't have a purpose for this pain, then this universe stinks.

Act 3: Rebellion

God gave Adam and Eve a single "Thou shalt not" in the midst of innumerable liberties. In Genesis 2 we encounter the Tree of the

Knowledge of Good and Evil, and it was from this tree only that they were forbidden to eat. Thousands upon thousands of trees bearing all varieties of fruits, and one tree from which they could not eat. If they ate of it, God declared that death would enter into creation.

All of a sudden, in the midst of what has been a story of *yes*, there appears a *no*. In the midst of a story all about life and creation, there appears mention of death. If they followed the voice of God, life would continue in peace and beauty, but should they rebel against His voice, it would lead to death.

Then comes a snake, a bite of fruit, and tremendous consequences.

> Now the serpent was more crafty than any other beast of the field that the Lord God had made. He said to the woman, "Did God actually say, 'You shall not eat of any tree in the garden'?" And the woman said to the serpent, "We may eat of the fruit of the trees in the garden, but God said, 'You shall not eat of the fruit of the tree that is in the midst of the garden, neither shall you touch it, lest you die.'" But the serpent said to the woman, "You will not surely die. For God knows that when you eat of it your eyes will be opened, and you will be like God, knowing good and evil." So when the woman saw that the tree was good for food, and that it was a delight to the eyes, and that the tree was to be desired to make one wise, she took of its fruit and ate, and she also gave some to her husband who was with her, and he ate. (Genesis 3:1–6)

The Bible doesn't say a lot about Satan.[10] We don't know much about his origin or the circumstances surrounding his appearance here in Eden. He just shows up as a talking serpent. He is a new voice in this story, a new character ("Satan" is a Hebrew word meaning "accuser"). So far all we have heard is the voice of God and Adam's response, but now there is a new voice. What will this voice say and how will Adam and Eve respond?

Attack

Straight away, Satan goes on a three-pronged attack against God and His words.

First, he questions and skews the very words of God. "Did God actually say, 'You shall not eat of any tree in the garden'?" He not only undermines the command, he exaggerates and twists it. God had said that they could eat of any tree *except* one, but in phrasing the question this way, Satan makes God out to sound like a curmudgeon who is withholding something from His people. In so doing, he plants the seed of doubt in the woman's mind.

Second, Satan turns up the heat and contradicts God's words directly. "You will not surely die," Satan tells her, but that's precisely the opposite of what God had said. God said, "You shall not eat of the fruit of the tree that is in the midst of the garden lest you die." Satan's second step was a full-frontal assault on God's command.

Finally, Satan outright lies. He says that God is not good. "God knows that when you eat of it your eyes will be opened, and you will be like God, knowing good and evil." By saying this he has painted a picture of a God who is withholding good from Eve, a God who does not want her to have the best and happiest. Only a God who is not good could possibly do such a thing.

By attacking in this way, the "father of lies" (John 8:44) masterfully changes Eve's focus. In this paradise of a million yeses and a single no, he manages to move Eve's mind from permission to prohibition. Her mind becomes fixated on the single thing to which God has said no.

Satan, despite all the centuries that have passed and all the changes in this world, has not changed a bit. He uses these exact same tactics today. He manipulates our minds and hearts to dwell on those things we cannot have, rather than on all the hopes and possibilities God has for us. Satan is real. He hates God, and he hates you. He hates truth and all who pursue it. Satan is the ultimate villain in history, and he is the villain of this story.

Bite = Brokenness

Many of us know the next part of the story. Eve bites fruit, Eve shares fruit, Adam bites fruit, and the rest is history. The first sin in human history was a simple bite, but a massive rebellion. Adam and Eve, the first people God created, turned against Him. God gave them all they could ever want, created them without flaw, and still they followed a different voice.

All the brokenness in this world, in your life, in your city, can be traced back to that simple bite. One taste of the forbidden fruit, and the world changed. Everything broke.

For Adam and Eve, things did not turn out quite like Satan had promised. Knowing Satan as we have come to know him in the several millennia since, that's not much of a surprise, but to them it must have been a horrific shock. He told them he could offer so much more than what God had offered. Instead, by following his voice, they lost so much of what God had given.

There is a battle between competing voices for the ear of all people. God speaks His truth, and Satan speaks his lies. To which will we respond? Ever since that fateful day in the garden, people are born predisposed to believe lies. We are born rebels. Our teeth marks are on that fruit just like Eve's. We would've done the same thing. Each of us has disregarded the voice of God and pursued the lie. And so we are all part of the brokenness.

Don't believe me? You don't think you'd do the same thing Adam and Eve did? Just look at this last week of your life. How often have you gone against what your conscience says is right this past week? Only the most prideful readers of this book would deny disregarding the voice of conscience and/or the voice of God this week. As foolish as their choice was, I think we're just like Adam and Eve. We would've made the same choice in the garden. It's what our own experience teaches us and it's what the Bible teaches us. As the old hymn declares, we're all "prone to wander."[11]

A Story That Makes Sense

I don't know about you, but this story makes sense to me. In my opinion, no other account of why this world is broken makes adequate sense. God creates a very good world where humans can flourish. He sets out rules to make it run and keep everything in its proper function and place. He gives very few laws, just one "Don't . . . or else"—don't disobey My voice or else this world will become unruled and unruly. But what do we do? We do the single thing we were told not to do. We rebel. For the first time, rebellion enters God's creation. And then comes pain and death where none had been before.

Think of a father, a good one, who has a teenage daughter. He loves her deeply and gives her everything she needs. He desires her happiness and well-being; he takes care of her every want and concern. Her life is one of a million yeses.

This good father offers only a single no. See, he knows that some young men are dangerous drivers. Some drink before driving and give no thought to how their actions could hurt others. With this in mind, he tells his daughter, "Never, ever get in the car with a boy who has been drinking."

What does this daughter do? She ignores her father's one warning, his one prohibition. She gets into the car with a boy who has been drinking. She bites the fruit. In the end, she is badly hurt in a car accident. It makes sense. She went against the voice of her father, and the consequences were real.

God too gave one rule to protect His people, one prohibition. They rebelled, and so have we. And now we suffer the pain.

Lawmaking

What drove that original sin was the same thing that has driven every sin since. Adam and Eve decided what was right in their own eyes. They chose *not* to live by faith and chose *not* to trust God's word. They went their own way, not God's way.

Sin is not just lawbreaking. Sin is also lawmaking. Adam and Eve didn't just break God's rules, they made up their own rules. They sought to be the god of their own lives. They would eat that fruit if they pleased. No one would tell them otherwise. That was their law.

We are exactly the same, just dressed differently. We ignore God's voice because we like the sound of our own voice. We ignore God's rule because we want to make our own rules. Don't believe me? Then you must not have any kids. Parenting makes you see that from the day your child is born, he or she is "prone to wander," prone to break your rules in order to make their own rules. We call it rebellion.

Naked . . . and Ashamed

Adam and Eve had been naked their whole life. They were created naked and lived naked. At the time of their creation, this was celebrated. They "were both naked and were not ashamed" (Genesis 2:25) in each other's presence and in God's presence.

Then came the serpent, then the bite of fruit, and this: "Then the eyes of both were opened, and they *knew* that they were naked. And they sewed fig leaves together and made themselves loincloths" (Genesis 3:7). For the first time in their lives, Adam and Eve *felt* naked.

This is the first experience in human history of shame and insecurity. It's the first time there was guilt and a loss of innocence.

We can barely remember losing our innocence. There was a time when we toddled through life, naked and uncaring. It was a time before we were conscious of our own flaws and sins and others' flaws and sins. We hadn't hurt anyone or been hurt bad enough to notice. We weren't self-aware enough. Then, one day, that innocence went away. That happened a long time ago for most of us. It went away when we began to taste the pain this world inflicts on us and that we inflict on others.

When we feel shame, what do we do? We do exactly what Adam and Eve did. We hide. Once they felt naked, once they felt the foreign presence of guilt and shame, Adam and Eve hid from God by standing behind a tree and covering themselves with fig leaves. They ran for the shrubbery and made themselves fig-leaf boxer shorts to cover the shame, to hide their true selves.

That was their strategy. Hiding. Hiding from God behind some leaves.

Here are the first two people created in the image of God, using the creation He made for their good to hide from Him. Man and woman were made for fellowship with God, to walk and talk with Him, not to hide from Him.

This is what sin does. It breaks the relationship between humanity and God. It breaks the relationship between people, too. Adam and Eve were hiding from God, sure, but they were hiding from one another as well. And they were hiding from their own selves. Sin is so insidious, it even breaks our relationship with our very self. We become insecure, ill at ease, unsure of who we really are, unable to face our own nakedness and shame.

Failing Fig Leaves

We all have our version of fig leaves we use to attempt to cover our failings, flaws, and sins. They can be hard to spot. We are master hiders, most of us. One effective way to determine what our fig leaves are is to ask, "What do I do on a regular basis to try to prove myself?" Or, "What masks do I wear?" What are those accomplishments or lies we are hiding behind to keep anyone from seeing the broken, ashamed sinner inside?

For some, it's intellect or a quick wit. For some, it's a polished, exquisite sense of style. For others, it's a carefree vibe they throw out. Sometimes it's work success, like closing a deal; or maybe you want to prove yourself with recreational excellence, such as a nice handicap in your golf game. They're all just fig leaves in the end.

That's how sick sin is; it fools us into thinking we can hide from God with our masks. But our fig leaves can't fix the pain. They may mask the pain for a short time, but they fix nothing—not the sin or the guilt or the shame. We're still naked and afraid.

Sin is like a malignant tumor, one we are born with. It spreads and spreads with a voracious need to conquer new flesh, to take over what was meant to be healthy. It's what is wrong with the whole world—original sin. We are all equally sick. We all have the cancer. And our fig leaves aren't fixing it.

A Pursuing God

Adam and Eve created a game called "hide." We still like to play this one today. But it was God who completed the game, created a better game, by adding the "seek."

God is a pursuing God. We sin against Him and rebel, but He pursues us. God always makes the first move toward a relationship with us.

In Genesis 3:9, God sets out to pursue Adam. "But the Lord God called to the man and said to him, 'Where are you?'" It's interesting that He asks for Adam, not Eve. He is aiming at the man to start. God proceeds to ask three questions.

Question 1: "Where are you?" (Genesis 3:9)

You think God didn't know? Of course He knew, but this is an opportunity for Adam to repent. Satan's voice lured Adam into sin, and it's going to take a stronger voice to bring him back out. This is no mere geographical question; it's a significant query about life. Through this question, we too can take stock of life. Where am I? What am I hiding from?

Question 2: "Who told you that you were naked?" (Genesis 3:11)

Again, this second question is for Adam's benefit. This is an opportunity for Adam to take stock of the consequences caused by his sin, to assess the cause of his newly felt nakedness.

Question 3: "Have you eaten of the tree of which I commanded you not to eat?" (Genesis 3:11)

Another chance for Adam to come clean, but what does Adam say in response? He blames Eve by saying, and I paraphrase, "No, that woman you gave me, she made me do it." Just a chapter earlier, when Adam first saw Eve, he was gushing poetry in praise of her and God. Now he turns on them both. He blames God and he blames Eve for his sin.

Now God turns to the woman with a fourth question: "What is this that you have done?" Eve, hearing Adam dump all the blame on her, realizes that two can play this game, so she turns and blames the serpent. Nobody will take responsibility for their actions. Adam and Eve are blame passers; they were the first people ever to claim that infamous status of "victim." It was her fault, it was the snake's fault, but it's definitely not *my* fault.

Apparently rebelling against God is nobody's fault. It's the first ever case of victimitis. It sounds a lot like how my wife and I argue—passing the blame instead of taking responsibility.

Excusers and Sinners

There's a big difference between excusers and sinners. God forgives sinners, but He wants nothing to do with excusers. C. S. Lewis has this to say about forgiveness and excuses:

> I find that when I think I am asking God to forgive me I am often in reality (unless I watch myself very carefully) asking Him to do something quite different. I am asking Him not to forgive me but to excuse me. But there is all the difference in

the world between forgiving and excusing. . . . If one was not really to blame then there is nothing to forgive. In that sense forgiveness and excusing are almost opposites . . . the trouble is that what we call "asking God's forgiveness" very often really consists in asking God to accept our excuses . . . we shall go away imagining that we have repented and been forgiven when all that has really happened is that we have satisfied ourselves with our own excuses . . . we are all too easily satisfied about ourselves. All the real excusing He will do. What we have got to take to Him is the inexcusable bit, the sin.[12]

We set out at the beginning of this chapter to discover where all the pain in this world came from. After looking at the story and thinking about ourselves, we have to be honest. We all have something to do with the pain and brokenness. Our sin, our rebellion, our choices have all contributed. Blaming and buck-passing solve nothing. Excuses get us nowhere. We must look at ourselves and recognize our unique contributions to the brokenness and pain in this world.

In 1908, *The Times* of London sent a question to a number of writers and journalists asking them to write an essay in response. The question was, "What is wrong with the world?" The plan was to run a feature story with these responses with the intention of getting some well-articulated and thought-out answers and maybe a bit of controversy. One of the people they sent the question to was G. K. Chesterton, the famous novelist and essayist. His response consisted of just two words:

"I am."[13]

To be a Christian is to give that answer; it's where the Christian life starts. As you hear God calling out to you, "Where are you?"

you are able to understand that you're a rebel and that what is wrong with the world has a lot to do with you. Is there more to it than this? Yes. What's wrong with this world must certainly include a long essay on the massacre at Sandy Hook Elementary School, and you didn't do that; such evil is likely far from your mind. But let's start right here, with you. No more blaming. No more excuses.

The Judgment Dilemma

For righteousness and justice to reign in this universe, God must clean up our mess. He must get rid of evil. It is judgment, a verdict and punishment, that does this removal. And it presents us with a dilemma because the world we all want, one without evil and suffering, requires judgment. Every time we see the bullets and the cancer and the horror and are pleading and crying out, "God do something! Change it! Fix it!" we are asking God for a brand-new world.

The good news is that God will do something. He has. We are getting to that part of the story. The dilemma, though, is that He must judge us, our sin, our part in creating this mess. The world we all want requires judgment, but that means God must also judge us.

Back to Genesis 3. What happens next is shocking. In a story that has been all about blessing, countless gifts, and freedom, we encounter a curse. A blessing means that someone has a future, a hope, good things coming. A curse means he will be cut off, the end will come, no hope. What once was a story looking toward hope and happiness now runs into the dead end of curse.

But God does not curse Adam and Eve. Instead, He judges

them. He promises that their rebellion will bring about very real, very painful consequences. He does not, however, say that their end is near, that their line will be cut off.

God only curses the serpent. He promises that the serpent, Satan, will meet his demise. There will be an end to evil. So even as God judges humanity, His curse on the devil offers them hope.

What was this judgment God handed down to Adam and Eve, if not a curse? It was pain. God gives the first man and woman pain where it will hurt them most, in the most sensitive areas of life. To Eve He gives pain in family, marriage, childbearing, and relationships. To the man He gives pain in his work. God gave man and woman pain in those arenas of life where men and women tend to seek their significance and identity.

Why did God do it this way?

The Purpose of Pain

After the judgment was handed down, God drove Adam and Eve from the garden and, ever since, life has been lived east of Eden. We live in a hard world, full of pain. It is foolish to pretend otherwise. We need not hide behind happy songs and hobbies. We ought not ignore the reality of our world. Life hurts.

But what if pain was given to us as a gift? What if this judgment wasn't vindictive?

Lepers wish they could feel pain. If a person has leprosy, she loses feeling progressively from extremities to the limbs. Without feeling pain, a leper may easily break a bone or suffer a gash and not even know it. No pain means that serious wounds go untreated, even those that might lead to death.

A thousand times a day, the normal person does something

that is harmful or potentially harmful to the body, and the body sends messages saying: stop. But somebody with Hansen's disease [leprosy] never receives those messages, unable to avoid the harm. . . . Consider the reason so many people with Hansen's disease go blind. When the eye functions properly, it has this marvelous capacity to clean and lubricate itself. Our blink reflex activates this healing; it's triggered by pain. We sense slight, almost subliminal pains, when our eyes start to dry out or we get stuff in them. If we stop feeling pain in the eye, we stop blinking, and our eyes dry out, gunk accumulates, our vision turns cloudy, and we rub our eyes, which causes abrasions and leads to infection. Before you know it, you lose your eye.[14]

So it is in our lives. Pain is a strange gift from God. It drives us back to Him. Without pain, we'd be fooled into thinking there is fulfillment away from His presence. Pain keeps us from taking God's good gifts (a spouse, a child, a job) and turning to them for ultimate fulfillment.

God sent Adam and Eve out of Eden, not just to punish, but to save them from the horrid reality of being eternally fallen. To stay in the garden was to live forever, so for them to stay would have meant an eternity of guilt, shame, nakedness, and hiding. Expulsion from the garden was a mercy.

Pain keeps a person from bleeding to death from an unrecognized wound, and it keeps a person from eternal death. It wakes us up to the reality that God created this world, and that we were made to know Him. We can thank God for pain. Pain reminds us that living life apart from God will lead to eternal separation. And so something must be done.

We can't fix this pain or hide it with fig leaves. Instead, we face this judgment dilemma. We want a better world, a perfect one, but the only way that can happen is through judgment. We are the ones who must be judged, but we don't want judgment. So what does God do?

The Serpent Crusher

Here we pick up the story again. Even as God tells Adam and Eve they must leave the garden, He doesn't send them empty-handed and naked. God makes clothes for them to warm and protect them. But He is meeting more than just a temporal need by covering their bodies; He is covering their guilt and shame because they will need a covering in order to enter His presence.

This is the first act of atonement in the Bible.

A sacrifice happens here. God sheds the blood of an innocent animal in order to cover His people. There is no appearing in the presence of God without covering, without something to shelter us from His glory—not in our sinful state. But even this sacrifice is not enough; it's symbolic. This sacrifice and every one thereafter foreshadow the great sacrifice yet to come.

Think back to a bit earlier in the story, Genesis 3:15. "I will put enmity between you and the woman, and between your offspring and her offspring; he shall bruise your head, and you shall bruise his heel." Theologians call this the "protoevangel"—the first gospel. From the line of the woman will come a descendant who will crush the serpent. Adam and Eve will go on, they will bear progeny, and one of these will defeat and abolish this devil and all evil along with it.

The rest of the Bible is the search for the serpent crusher, and throughout its pages, Satan does all he can to prevent Him from coming.

In Exodus (the second book of the Bible), Satan prompts Pharaoh to commit infanticide against all the Hebrew baby boys. But two midwives remained faithful to God, even at the risk of death, and preserved the life of one baby boy. God raises up this baby through incredible twists and turns to lead the people out of captivity and into the Promised Land. But even for all his great leadership, Moses was not the serpent crusher.

In 1 Samuel, Satan prods King Saul to try and pin a young man to the wall with a spear, but the young man escapes. For years, Saul pursues that same man with ruthless and pathological doggedness, seeking to kill him. Instead God raises the young man, David, to be the great king of Israel and father the line from which the serpent crusher would later come. So even David was not that man.

As generation after generation and king after king comes and goes in the nation of Israel (the nation by which God promised to make Himself known to the world), Satan leads the people into idolatry, away from the true God. He seeks to remove any chance of the new king's coming by dismantling the nation altogether, and he nearly succeeds. The people reject God for so long that eventually they are exiled from their home, the Promised Land. Foreign nations reign over them and remove them. For decades, they are refugees and aliens with no home, no temple, and a faith that is dashed. But even in this time, God raises up men like Daniel, Nehemiah, and Ezra, to lead the people home and restore His nation. But none of these men is the serpent crusher either.

Throughout the pages, Satan doesn't stop. In Matthew he moves King Herod to such jealousy that Herod commands that all the boys in Bethlehem under the age of two be slaughtered, lest one of them grow up to claim his throne. But God sends an angel to warn the father of a particular baby to flee, and flee he does. So the baby boy is saved.

And this particular baby grows into a man, a man named Jesus. And it was *this* man who had the calling and the courage to stand between mankind and all evil. He held His ground between us and the ravenous serpent and crushed its head with His heel. And in so doing, He took a fang in the foot, a fatal bite. Satan struck at the cross, and he thought he had won. It looked like the line of Eve was defeated. But this man was not like Moses or David or any other great leader.

Jesus is the serpent crusher, the promised one of Genesis 3. Satan had no power over Him. Death had no power over Him. He did die, but He did not stay dead. He rose from the dead after three days. Satan's poison had no hold on Him. Sin, death, and Satan were defeated on that day. Even as Satan, sin, and pain linger today, they are ultimately powerless over anyone who is with Jesus, who claims Him as their king.

Jesus crushed the serpent. He swallowed and took upon Himself all the pain in this world, so that one day we can live in a world where there is no pain. So that one day God could end evil and suffering without having to end you and me. Jesus was judged so that you and I don't have to be judged.

Theologian John Stott once said, "I could never myself believe in God if it were not for the cross. In the real world of pain, how could one worship a God who was immune to it?"[15] The God of the Bible is not immune to pain. Only Christianity gives you a God who suffers, a God who cares so much about you that He entered into our broken world, got involved with the mess, and suffered pain in order to take care of us. Why do evil and suffering continue in our world while we live in between Act 4 and Act 5, awaiting the second coming of Jesus? Why is my mom dying of cancer? Why were twenty children buried in Connecticut this week? I don't know. But I know that the answer *isn't* that God doesn't care. Only the Big Story tells of a God who cares, gets involved, and suffers in order to be with us. Our world is broken. But God is not. In Chapter 2, I said that the three most important things to know about God are that He is sovereign, wise, and good. Add a fourth truth to that list: God suffers. No other story says this. Plenty of other worldviews talk about *your* suffering, about the suffering you must go through to work your way to a god. Only Christianity tells you about *God's* suffering, that God suffered in order to work His way to you.

We are rebels. And so our world is full of pain.

Fortunately, God is a good and suffering God. And so He sent His only Son, the long-promised serpent crusher, to enter into the pain and rescue rebels.

Rescue. That's what the next chapter is all about.

STORY CONTRAST (REBELLION VS._____):
The Big Story explains that the brokenness in our world is a result of our rebellion against God. What stories do people around you believe to make sense out of the brokenness inside of them and around them? In what ways does the Big Story make better sense of the pain and brokenness?

ACTION STEP: Revisit your life story / life graph that you created at the end of Chapter 1. Many of the significant moments you graphed on your life story are moments of pain. In what ways do you see that these were strange gifts from God? How has pain been a gift in your life?

RECOMMENDED READING: Your local newspaper. Get a subscription to your local newspaper, read it regularly, and notice how most of the news is bad news—news about the pain and brokenness in our world. How can you process the bad news in your city or town with what you learned in this chapter?

"The gospel is not just a series of facts to which we yield our assent but a dramatic narrative that re-plots our identity."
—**Michael Horton**[1]

• • •

"I have heard your exhortations and they will not help me. Do you have good news for me?"
—**J. Gresham Machen**[2]

• • •

"While we are looking at God we do not see ourselves—blessed riddance. The man who has struggled to purify himself and has had nothing but repeated failures will experience real relief when he stops tinkering with his soul and looks away to the Perfect One."
—**A. W. Tozer**[3]

• • •

5

ACT 4:

RESCUE

Just as Satan would go to insane lengths to ensure the destruction of mankind and the defeat of all threats to himself, so God goes to impossible lengths to find, pursue, and rescue us when we are lost. So many times when Satan tried to destroy a threat, it was a threat that God put there.

The sacrifice of the animal in the garden of Eden was the earliest of what became an entire sacrificial system for His people over the years. Animals were slaughtered by priests in a ceremony at God's temple, and this wasn't just some grotesque ritual. The animals served as substitutes for the people, for the entire nation. All the people deserved punishment from God for their sins, but God provided a way of atonement by allowing them to substitute bulls and sheep. No animal could bear the ongoing sins of the people, so month after month, year after year, more animals were slaughtered. It was a mercy from God to the people. But this atonement was not complete. It represented a better sacrifice to come, one that would not need to be repeated, because the one sacrificed would be perfect.

And so we enter Act 4 of the Bible's story: Rescue. God sent Jesus, whose very name means "God saves," to be the Rescuer. He was the ultimate and perfect serpent crusher and sacrifice. He lived a perfect life, the kind of life none of us are capable of living. He died on the cross, dying the death we deserve to die, because of our rebellion against God. And He rose again from the dead and ascended to heaven, guaranteeing us life on the other side of death. Jesus is God's rescue plan.

Lost Sinners, Lost Saints

We know from the Genesis 3 story that we all are lost. All have been party to biting the apple. But there is not just a single way to be lost. In fact, there are two main ways to be lost, two main pits of alienation from God from which we need rescue. In one of His most famous parables (a story that is meant to give a message or lesson), Jesus tells a tale that clearly depicts these two paths of "lostness."

This story is told in Luke 15 (Luke is one of the four biographies written about the life, death, and resurrection of Jesus), and the chapter starts off nicely with a scandal. Jesus, this One we have called sinless, is hanging out with what the author called "tax collectors and sinners" (v. 1). This doesn't sound flattering, exactly, but neither does it sound too nasty to readers in a modern context. Take a look at what it meant to be a tax collector in the first-century Roman Empire.

These tax collectors were agents of Rome. That made them lackeys of the grand dictatorship that was so roundly hated by all of Israel. More than being representatives of Rome, they were thieves and scam artists. They would lie about what taxes people owed and take the extra for themselves. They got rich in the name of Rome and by fleecing the oppressed. Yet here Jesus was, hanging out with them.

And the rest of the crowd was not just the questionable sort. These were truly bad people. They were the sexually promiscuous and the prostitutes. They were those people who were flagrantly ruining their own lives and the lives of those around them. They were so publicly reckless and immoral that they were known simply as "sinners." And here sat Jesus.

And so it was that the Pharisees, those moral and religious leaders, those lawmakers and law enforcers, those pillars of Jewish uprightness, took issue with Him. To the Pharisees, such people were to be shunned, at best. Yet here in Luke 15:2, we see a striking irony. These same angry religious leaders unwittingly preach the gospel in their criticism: "This man receives sinners and eats with them."

Without meaning to, they summed up the truth of the gospel: that God the Son had come precisely to receive sinners and eat with them. He had come to bring them into relationship with Himself. In first-century Jewish culture, to sit down and eat with somebody was to accept them. It was to enter into a relationship with them. And that is exactly what Jesus was doing.

The Younger Son

When Jesus saw the Pharisees' reaction and heard their grumbling about Him, He told them a series of three parables about rescue, but one in particular stands out—the parable of the prodigal son. It is the story of a wealthy man with two sons. And this is how it begins:

> "There was a man who had two sons. And the younger of them said to his father, 'Father, give me the share of property that is coming to me.' And he divided his property between them. Not many days later, the younger son gathered all he had and took a journey into a far country." (Luke 15:11–13)

The younger son came to the father and demanded his inheritance. It's important to understand what this meant in its context. According to Old Testament law, the law all Jesus' listeners would have known, the oldest son of a family was to receive two-thirds of the entire inheritance, and the other sons would divide up the remaining third. So upon the father's death, this younger son would normally have received one-third of all his father had. But to ask for his portion while the father yet lived was a shameful, abhorrent thing to do; it was to openly wish that his father was dead and to look him in the face and tell his father that whatever property he was to receive was more valuable than the father's very life. The younger son basically told him, "I want you dead, and I want your money."[4]

I had a chance to preach through this parable while traveling and teaching in Cambodia. It was in a rural context, and the culture had many similarities to first-century agrarian societies like the one where our story is set. I asked the people what would happen if a son in their society came to his father and made the same demands as the younger son in our story did. Their response was quick and stark. The son would be beaten for his disrespect. Beyond that, if the father was wealthy, he would take out an article in a local paper or publication to definitively disown his son.

It wouldn't be at all surprising to see the same sort of reaction from the father in this parable. He had every right to hurt and shame this boy for his unconscionable disrespect. But what does the father do? He divides his property and gives the younger son his portion. He does the opposite of what culture called for. This father was willing to suffer a broken heart.

Of course the younger son is stricken with gratefulness to the father and shame for his actions. Right? Wrong. He takes the money and runs. He runs as far away as he can get, to a far country. And this is just what he wanted. He's out from under the thumb, out of his father's house, out of his older brother's shadow, and he has coin to spend. Life is going *his* way now.

When he gets to that far country, he sets himself up a business all on his own. He takes that inheritance and creates a new life for himself, a fresh start, a chance for prosperity. Right? Wrong. He lives a "reckless" life. He does what so many young folks do who leave home wanting nothing to do with Mom or Dad and want to be the god of their own lives. He wastes his inheritance. He ruins himself. He goes on one big Vegas-style bender, complete with lowlifes, prostitutes,[5] drunkenness, and all the other accoutrements. And he comes out of it friendless and broke.

Jesus tells the story this way with a purpose. He is describing sin. He describes fleeing from home, a place of love and security, to a faraway place in an effort to run your own life. He describes trying to make your own rules, rule your own life, do things your way. And what comes of it?

Famine comes upon the penniless young man. Again Jesus is prodding home a point. If you are a younger-son type, seeking your own way and rebelling, you need to realize something. Famine will come. It may already have come. Hard times, hard circumstances will come, and you will be brought to your knees, just as this young man is.

Pigs and Prepared Speeches

The younger son is in a desperate place. He has blown his entire inheritance. He is alone in a land where the only friends he had were those he bought and who stuck around until the booze ran out. And now there is a famine in the land, and he can't even come up with food to eat. So he hires himself out to the only employer he can find: a pig farmer. His job is to feed the pigs. He is a slop slinger.

But things go from bad to worse. This job isn't providing what he needs. The younger son is slowly starving. So he resorts to the only option that's left. He begins sharing the slop with the pigs. Day after day, he dines on soiled, spoiled scraps and refuse that truly is fit only for swine.

This is embarrassing and lowly for anyone of any culture, but for a Jewish boy this would have been truly shameful. Pigs were not just stinky, they were unclean by Jewish law. This means that they were not to be eaten, touched, or approached. But to eat alongside them at the trough? Utterly humiliating, even dehumanizing, especially for a Jewish boy who grew up in wealth and comfort. Remember, Jesus is telling this story to the religious leaders, the top theologians of the day, the church folk. He is describing a boy who is maximally unclean. He has shamed his father and, with that, brought shame to his whole family. He has squandered his wealth on prostitutes and all flavors of immorality. And now, not only is he caring for the most unclean of animals, they are his dinner companions.

As the younger son sits in this squalor, blanketed in shame, he begins to think about the servants from his father's house, the same ones who used to work for him. They all have a roof over their heads. They never go hungry. They get bread—real, fresh bread—yet here he sits, choking down pig slop. And so he begins to hatch a plan.

It starts with a speech in two parts. Part one of the speech lays the groundwork: "Father, I have sinned . . . I am no longer worthy to be called your son" (vv. 18–19a). Part two of the speech makes the request: "Treat me as one of your hired servants" (v. 19b). He is going to ask his father to take him back, but not as a son. He wants to come back as a servant and, over time, work toward paying back the debt he owes.

This kid still thinks money is the problem. After all he has been through, he still thinks his debt to his father is financial. The issue isn't that money has been lost. It's that *he* is lost.

Homecoming

These next scenes should stay vivid in our minds for the rest of our lives. The son has made the long journey home. Who knows how he has eaten or found shelter along the way, but here he is, approaching the town where he grew up. He trudges up the long, dusty road leading to the village. The houses on either side are close together with a wall surrounding the whole town for protection, not unlike so many other Middle Eastern towns of those days. The wall has only one opening, a gate, and through this the younger son walks up the main street, through the heart of this town.

He looks the part of poverty and famine. He smells the part of pigs and slop, with a sprinkling of sweat and a coat of dirt from the road. He is emaciated and filthy. He slumps; his head hangs. He is ashamed and afraid. He exudes hopelessness. There is no doubt that he will face the scorn and ridicule of his neighbors. He braces for the curses, the spittle, and the stones. All he holds to is the thinnest thread of hope that his father might, *just maybe*, take him on as a servant.

As he approached the village, he would have fully expected the villagers to ridicule him and even beat him—a customary way of handling citizens who had brought so much shame and disrepute upon a fellow family in the village. He also would have expected his father to be about his business in the house while all this judgment took place.

But as he comes into view of his father's home, amazing things transpire.

Five Life-Changing Verbs

A verb is an action word, something being done. They are words that make a story go, the backbone and force of a narrative. In verse 20, we see five verbs that change the younger son's life forever.

> "But while he was still a long way off, his father *saw* him and *felt compassion*, and *ran* and *embraced* him and *kissed* him."
> (Luke 15:20)

First, the father *saw* his son. He was looking for him. He hadn't given up on him. He was waiting, hoping his boy would come home. He saw him because he was awaiting the first opportunity to do so. This is no small thing, considering the way the boy turned tail and abandoned the family. But the father never abandoned his hope for his son's return.

Then the father *felt compassion*. This story was originally written in Greek and later translated into English. Sometimes there are potent word pictures in the Greek that tell us the story even better than English can. This is one of those times. The Greek word that is translated as "compassion" is *splankna*, something you feel in your guts, down in that deepest place of emotion. This is almost a physical reaction and sensation of being broken up and torn apart, but in a tender way, a sympathetic way. He responds not with bitterness, fury, or coldness. He responds with *splankna*, with gut-churning compassion for his son.

What the father does next is particularly startling. He *runs* to his son. He gathers up his long robes in his hands, and sprints. For a middle-aged man of first-century Jewish culture, this was most undignified. Children ran. Animals ran. Men did not run. But all that *splankna* he felt deep inside came rushing out, and he picked up the hems of his robes and ran to his boy, because dignity is no match for deepest love and compassion. As one scholar states:

> In the Middle East a man of his age and position *always* walks in a slow, dignified fashion. It is safe to assume that he has not run anywhere for any purpose for forty years. No villager over the age of twenty-five ever runs. But now the father *races* down the road. To do so, he must take the front edge of his robes in his hand like a teenager. When he does this, his legs

show in what is considered a humiliating posture. All of this is painfully shameful for him. The loiterers in the street will be distracted from tormenting the prodigal and will instead run after the father, amazed at seeing this respected village elder shaming himself publicly. It is his "compassion" that leads the father to race out to his son. He knows what his son will face in the village. He takes upon himself the shame and humiliation due the prodigal.[6]

What many people miss in this parable is the sacrifice and humiliation that comes from the father's act of running to his son. It represents what God incarnate has done for us: God doesn't wait for prodigals to come to Him. Instead God takes the initiative to run after sinners and takes upon Himself the shame and humiliation that sinners deserve so that the sinner may be set free and forgiven. This is the heart of Christianity.

And when this man of dignity (or man of former dignity), this respected member of society, reaches his son, what does he do? He *embraces* his son. This nasty, emaciated, pig-smelling, dust- and sweat-covered kid gets wrapped in the loving arms of his father. And this is not a mere "Nice to see you" hug with a pat on the back, or a polite side hug. No, the father envelops the son in a rib-crunching, lung-compressing embrace of sheer love.

You've heard the phrase "sealed with a kiss," and that is what the father does last. He *kisses* his son. As if the embrace wasn't enough, he plants a kiss on the boy's dirty face. I often give my sons "smackers," those good, big, sloppy kisses that show just how much I love them. I don't know if this was a smacker or not, but it was, without a doubt, a kiss the son never forgot.

Change

Now we see a change come over the son. That two-part speech he so carefully planned and strategized, the one that had once seemed like his best possible option, no longer seems to make sense. What had made sense in the far country doesn't make sense in the father's arms. This reception—the running, the eagerness, the embrace, and the kiss—has shown him clearly that his plan is no longer the right one. He is beginning to understand the depths of his own "lostness." It's clear now that he owes a debt he can never repay, far beyond any amount of money. He has looked into the depths of his father's love for him.

The son has finally started to understand grace, and he responds to his father differently than planned. He delivers the first part of his speech, "Father I have sinned against heaven and before you. I am no longer worthy to be called your son" (v. 21), and that's where he stops. The second part of his speech, the part about earning his keep and paying his father back, has become irrelevant and inadequate. He simply confesses his utter failure and casts himself upon his father's mercy. Experiencing the father's kiss changed his speech and changed his heart.

And mercy pours forth. The father's response is incredible. He doesn't berate or chastise or reprimand. No, he calls for gifts to be brought. Immediately, the father gives four gifts to his son.

First is the father's own robe. Walking through the village with the father's robe, this robe would communicate to the villagers that this prodigal had been reinstated into the family. Second, the son is given a ring—the signet ring of the family—yet another symbol of reinstatement. Third, the gift of shoes. In that culture slaves went barefoot, but sons wore shoes. All those mocking neighbors and townsfolk will see just whose son this is and what family he is part of. He is wrapped in the father's care, literally and figuratively, and has been given the symbol of the house. The disgusting swineherd has been transformed from rags and rot to robes and rings—from slave to son again.

Parties and Party Poopers

What the father calls for next, though, takes this from a sweet homecoming to a whole other level. He calls for the fattened calf. This was the family's most precious animal—specially fed and protected—kept for the most special of occasions. When butchered and prepared, it could feed seventy-five or more people. Well, if there was that much food, why not invite the whole village? That's what this father does. Now, this is a big party, and the father reminds everyone in attendance why they're celebrating: because "my son was dead, and is alive again; he was lost, and is found" (v. 24). Incidentally, earlier in this chapter, Jesus says this is what happens in heaven anytime someone is rescued and begins to believe the Big Story: a party is thrown in heaven. "Just so, I tell you, there will be more joy in heaven over one sinner who repents than over ninety-nine righteous persons who need no repentance" (v. 7).

The party is in full swing. Drinks are flowing, music is blasting, people are hitting the dance floor. But let's turn our attention to someone else, someone we were introduced to, ever so briefly, at the very beginning of this story but have heard nothing from since: the older son.

He is working out in the field, finishing up a long day of hard work. As he packs it in and heads toward home, he hears the sounds of music and partying, so he calls to a servant to find out what is going on. The servant, caught up in the excitement of the celebration, eagerly announces, "Your brother has come, and your father has killed the fattened calf, because he has received him back safe and sound" (v. 27). Notice that the father in this parable is doing exactly what Jesus was doing at the start of our chapter (vv. 1–2), eating with sinners! The religious leaders were infuriated that Jesus was feasting with sinners. And this brother feels the same way about what's happening in his family.

At this point, you can almost hear the tires screeching, as the joyous emotions skid to a sudden halt. The older brother is infuriated. He refuses to even enter the party. There is no way in God's green earth he will celebrate the return of that no-good loser of a brother. Why?

Because the older brother is just as lost as his younger brother was. No, he never left home. He never shamed his family. He never ran off to run his own life. He has kept every rule. But he is lost. This brother, too, is alienated from the father. He too has a broken relationship with the father. He too needs healing. His brokenness just looks different—this brother thought he'd earned a relationship with the father through hard work and obedience. This brother thinks he's deserved what can only be given by grace: a relationship with the father.

He won't enter the party because he doesn't want grace. To him, life is all about what a person deserves and what he earns. Grace has no place in his economy of goodness. So the older brother throws his own pity party outside of the real party. For some people, grace isn't amazing, it's infuriating. The elder brother is angry that his brother didn't pay the price for his rebellion, angry that his father paid the price for his brother. This son sees that his brother has been reinstated into the family through the father's costly, countercultural grace.

In the midst of his self-righteous fervor, the older brother has done something shameful too. As the oldest son, he was the first representative of the family, of his father's wishes. He was expected to uphold all that his father asked of him and expected. And even as he blathers and blusters about how well he has done this, he was failing at it. By refusing to enter the party, he too has shamed his father and his family name.

> The older son's response is crucially significant. He refuses to enter the banquet hall where the guests have already arrived. In any social situation . . . the male members of the family must come and shake hands with the guests even if they don't stay and visit. They cannot stay aloof if they are anywhere in the vicinity of the house. Failure to fulfill this courtesy is a personal insult to the guests and to the father, as host. The older son knows this and thereby his action is an intentional public insult to his father. . . . This is an open rupture of relationship between the son and his father. The situation is very serious because all this takes place publicly during a banquet. Because it is in public, this rebellion of the older son is more serious than the earlier rebellion of the prodigal.[7]

More Grace, More Rebellion

The poor father. As he welcomes home one lost son who he thought never to see again, he is affronted by his other. In that culture this father would've had every right to, would've been expected to, have his son dragged into the party and reprimanded in front of all of the guests. How does the father respond? For the second time in the same day, this father goes out to a lost son.

The father leaves the party, walks out to his son, and entreats him to enter. He speaks tenderly and cajoles with care. The father knows this son has a hard time with grace, so he seeks to reason with him. He explains the party and the significance of the younger brother's return. He seeks to persuade the older brother that it would be so much better to be inside, celebrating with everyone else. The father is appealing to his son's heart, not demanding that he act a certain way. The father had already been shamed by his son's refusal to join the party; now he's bearing even more shame by deliberately leaving his guests to humbly stand outside and love, forgive, and entreat his son.

But the elder brother will have none of it. He cuts his father off mid-sentence and launches into a speech of his own, a speech that reveals just what is in his heart.

> "Look, these many years *I* have served you, and *I* never disobeyed your command, yet you never gave *me* a young goat, that *I* might celebrate with *my* friends. But when this son of yours came, who has devoured your property with prostitutes, you killed the fattened calf for him!" (vv. 29–30)

The older son doesn't even have the courtesy to address his father; he rudely begins his speech with "Look." At least the younger son had the courtesy to begin his speech with "Father." In first-century Jewish culture, it was extremely rude to not use a title when speaking to someone who was your senior. And then comes the first "I," one of many first-person pronouns that dominate the elder son's speech. His logic is the logic of many of our hearts; it's the logic of religion, not grace: "God, I've served You. I've done everything right. I deserve better. You owe me."

Remember how back in the far country, the younger son had a two-part speech, but how in the father's arms of grace, he dropped the second part of his speech? The second part of his speech was about being a servant who could earn the father's favor: "Treat me as a hired servant." For his whole life, the elder brother has been living part two of his brother's speech—he's spent his whole life laboring as a servant, trying to earn his way. He's always been a servant, never a son. He's kept the rules, he's worked hard, and now he thinks he deserves better.

His speech is also full of lies, such as never having a young goat in order to feast with his friends. The elder son would've already received two-thirds of the father's inheritance. His whole life, he's been surrounded by his father's provision, his father's stuff, his father's feast. This son had everything. But he's been living in famine. He's never come into the feast. His self-righteousness has prevented him from enjoying the grace all around him.

The final sentence of his speech is one of comparison. Elder-brother types are always calculating and comparing. The elder son states his superiority to his younger brother, enraged that his brother has received supposed better treatment from the father. The elder son believes that he has earned what his brother has received by grace—the calf, the robe, and the kiss. Elder-brother types think that they have to earn their acceptance with God, and that others have to earn it too. Most of the world's religions fit into elder-brother living. Elder-brother religions—Islam, Hinduism, Buddhism, and others—these ask you to pull up your bootstraps, work hard, and earn your way to Allah, nirvana, or good karma.

See, it's pride that kept the elder brother from ever experiencing his father's kiss. The Big Story, Christianity, calls us to repent, not just of the pride of running off to the far country to break all the rules (like the younger son), but also the pride of staying in the near country, keeping all the rules, and thinking that gets us a relationship with God. Pastor Tim Keller puts it this way:

> Irreligious people seek to be their own saviors and lords through irreligion, "wordly" pride. ("No one tells me how to live or what to do, so I determine what is right and wrong for me!") But moral and religious people seek to be their own saviors and lords through religion, "religious" pride. ("I am more moral and spiritual than other people, so God owes me to listen to my prayers and take me to heaven. God cannot let just anything happen to me—he owes me a happy life. I've earned it!") The irreligious person rejects Jesus entirely, but the religious person only uses Jesus as an example and helper and teacher—but not as a Savior. These are two different ways to do the same thing—control our own lives. . . . Christians are people who come to see that *both* their sins *and* their best deeds have all really been ways of avoiding Jesus as savior.[8]

If we're not like the younger son, we're like the older son. Whether through an outwardly prideful life of breaking the rules or an inwardly prideful life of keeping the rules, we are people who have sought to avoid Jesus and run our own lives.

The father's response, yet again, is grace. The very end of this story is his response to his older son. "And he said to him, 'Son, you are always with me, and all that is mine is yours. It was fitting to celebrate and be glad, for this your brother was dead, and is alive; he was lost, and is found'" (vv. 31–32). He essentially says, "Son, grace has been yours every day that you have been with me, and now your brother is home and grace is his too." There is grace for the unrighteous and the self-righteous alike, and the father loves both sons well.

Two Ways Lost, One Way Saved

Through this story, Jesus makes it clear that there are two ways to be lost. They look very different but are equally lost. There is the younger son, and it's easy to see those who emulate him. Maybe you've been that person. This one is determined to run his own life, to do things his way. He says, loud and proud, "Forget You, God." It is a rebel's life and it is obvious.

The other way is that of the older son, and it is subtle. It is to be the goody two-shoes, to do the right things and keep all the rules. If you are this son, you think that your excellent behavior has earned a relationship with God. You think that He owes it to you, as if such a thing can be earned. In this life, grace is a threatening thing, something to be kept away. It makes you angry. Why does it make you so angry? Because grace means there are three words you can never say to God: "You owe me." Grace destroys entitlement. But grace is the foundation of the Christian life. The younger son broadcasts his need for it. The older son hides his. But the need is equal.

Jesus tells this story as He travels to Jerusalem, the seat of religious power in Israel, the home of the Pharisees. It is the seat of all legal and legalistic power. It is a brood of older brothers. The people listening to this parable are the same people who in a short time will scream, "Crucify Him! Crucify Him!" and gloat as Jesus is nailed, innocent, to a plank of wood and raised up on the cross.

And it is there on the cross that we see what this Christian life is built on. As Jesus looks down on these enraged faces, the gloating ones, the victorious ones, what does He say? Does He curse them, as is His right? Does He announce their guilt to the world? Instead, He says the unthinkable. He gives the best speech of all: "Father, forgive them, for they know not what they do" (Luke 23:34). To be a Christian is to bank your life on this speech of grace.

To be a Christian is to do away with the speech and pride of the older son, thinking you have earned the favor of God. It is to realize that you need to be ruled by God, not be your own god. Supremely, it is to hang your whole life on the words of Jesus on the cross, where He suffered for sins of younger son types and elder son types alike, "Father, forgive them, for they know not what they do."

A Double-Beamed Life

I have a tattoo on my wrist. I got it when I was twenty-one. I went out for burgers with my brother, Mark, and we decided to get them together. It was sort of a brotherly thing to do. It's a tattoo of a cross. I know that might seem cliché, but it has eternal and infinite significance for my life. I got it so that every time I would look down at my arm, I would see the two beams of the cross, and it would remind me what Jesus has done for me. And what He has called me to be in this world.

The cross has two beams, one vertical and one horizontal. The vertical beam points to heaven and earth. It reminds us that our relationship with God has been reconciled and restored only through what Jesus did on that cross. We were lost, whether like the younger son or the older son. We could not find ourselves, find joy, or find God. We were dead inside, totally hopeless.

It is only through what Jesus has done that we can have a relationship with God. Through Jesus, the relationship that broke in the garden of Eden is restored to new again. Our sins can be forgiven. That debt we owe, the one the younger son thought he could pay back, cannot be paid. Not ever. Our debt is like an empty ocean bed, and all the philanthropy, social service, social justice, creative production, and other human effort we can give would be a drop of water. But Jesus did pay it, and He was the only one who could do so. He paid with His life, the final and perfect sacrifice to end all sacrifices. And He sealed it with His resurrection. And that is what the vertical beam reminds us of.

Then there is the second beam, the horizontal one. It reminds us of our connectedness to the world around us, billions of broken people who don't yet know God. They don't yet know this Jesus who can restore their relationship with God. Many have never even heard the name Jesus. They don't know the God who saves younger and older sons alike.

This beam reminds us that followers of Jesus, those who know the reality of His grace, are called to go into the world and help these people know that same grace, to know Jesus. Followers of Jesus should be a community that is like the party from this parable—a celebration of grace that draws people in with joy, hope, and gladness.

Each one of us is a prodigal. We have all been lost, maybe still are. But Jesus came for us, not with a bold knock at the door and loud announcement of, "I'm here!" Instead He sent someone—a friend, a family member, a coworker, a stranger—or maybe this book—to introduce you to Him. That person brought you to the party. And it should be a celebration of changed lives. Each of us ought to be so happy that Jesus found us and saved us, that we are running to find the next person who needs to be introduced to Him. That's what the church is, a community of rescued people celebrating grace, eager to spread the good news of grace and bring other people into the party.

> Grace aims at the celebration of life: "Let us eat, and be merry: for this my son was dead, and is alive again; he was lost, and is found." Indeed, Grace is the celebration of life, relentlessly hounding all the non-celebrants in the world. It is a floating, cosmic bash shouting its way through the streets of the universe, flinging the sweetness of its cassations to every window, pounding at every door in a hilarity beyond all liking and happening, until the prodigals come out at last and dance, and the elder brothers finally take their fingers out of their ears.[9]

Lost, Found, Rescued

Lost. That's what every person is without Jesus. *Found*. That's what we are when Jesus brings us into the celebration of His grace. *Rescued*. That's what we are forever, in Jesus. We are rescued from ourselves, our own self-destruction. We are rescued from the judgment we earned through our rebellion. We are rescued from the wrath of God, which is rightly poured out on those who refuse the gracious work of Jesus.

Undeserved love. This is the only thing that has ever deeply changed me. Other stories offer self-help programs. The Big Story offers rescue.

STORY CONTRAST (RESCUE VS._____): The Big Story says that the best news in the world is news of rescue— that the secret to life is being rescued and receiving grace, instead of futilely working hard to save yourself. What stories do people around you believe about how to fix the brokenness inside of them and around them? In what ways does the Big Story make better sense out of how to fix the deep brokenness?

ACTION STEP: Whether you believe it or not, talk about the message of this chapter with some of your friends.

RECOMMENDED READING: Galatians. Galatians is a short book in the New Testament that articulates the message of Rescue arguably better than any other book in the Bible. Read and reread Galatians for the next month or two or three of life. Soak in this book. Get the message of Galatians into your bones.

6

INTERMISSION

At this point, I think it's important to take a brief intermission, especially for those of you not as well acquainted with the road to Jesus. There are common misconceptions and vital details you need to know about.

This rescuing we've been talking about, it's not just offered to special people. It's offered to you, no matter who you are, where you live, or what you've done. You also need to understand that talking to God, telling Him you are desperate for grace, will bring about a lot of change in your life. It doesn't mean you have to live life perfectly and always do the right thing; you couldn't even if you wanted to. But God will still love you. And you will notice a change in yourself. If this doesn't quite make sense to you, read through this intermission.

It will also be a valuable intermission for those who have

already made a decision to say yes to Jesus. After this, we'll continue into Act 5: Home.

The Call

Remember in elementary school, at recess or in gym class when you needed to pick teams to play a sport, and everyone would line up and select two captains, and the captains would pick teams? What a tense experience that was. The biggest thrill of all was to be the *first* pick. It meant that, for *that* recess at least, you were the best player. It meant that the captain thought you would give his team the best chance of winning.

But who was it that Jesus picked first? In Mark 1 (this is the passage we looked at in Chapter 1) we saw that it was Simon, also known as Peter. At first blush, this doesn't seem very surprising since he went on to gain fame as "Saint Peter," write two books of the Bible, and be one of the founders of the Christian church. But at the time Jesus picked him? Not so much.

When Jesus initially walked up to Peter and said, "Follow me," Peter was a young man, probably in his late teens or early twenties. He was a fisherman, not a scholar or professionally trained in anything. And from that point on, he was a constant screwup all through Jesus' ministry. Peter's failures reached their peak when he lied and cursed and abandoned Jesus when Jesus needed him most, at the time of His trial before being killed. Peter was a total mess. And Peter was Jesus' first pick!

What could be more encouraging than realizing that Jesus calls the unqualified? If Peter, a messy, impulsive adolescent, could be Jesus' choice to lead His disciples, we should have great hope. You don't need to submit an impressive resume to get a relationship with Jesus. And there are no strings attached. Jesus, of all the possible masters and lords in the world, is the One who will love you even when you fail Him. In other areas of life, you fail and get beat up for it, you suffer the consequences. Not with Jesus.

Our relationship with Jesus is based on grace—on the unexpected, undeserved, counterintuitive love of God. Grace is different than what we're used to. The math works differently. Martin Lloyd-Jones, a Welsh preacher who ministered during the first half of the twentieth century, says this about God's outrageous grace:

> It is God's accountancy. He's always giving us surprises. You never know what he's going to do. His bookkeeping is the most romantic thing I know of in the world. Our ledgers are out of date. They're of no value. We're in the kingdom of God and it's God's accountancy. It's all of grace. It's grace at the beginning. Grace at the end. So when you and I come to lie upon our deathbeds, the one thing that should comfort and help and strengthen us there is the thing that helped us at the beginning. Not what we have been. Not what we've done. But the grace of God in Jesus Christ our Lord. The Christian life starts with grace, it must continue with grace, it ends with grace. Grace, wondrous grace.[1]

Whether for the first time or the thousandth time, I want you to hear the call of Jesus, enjoy the love of Jesus, and follow Jesus. Following Him is following a good master, the *one* good master. He will love you even when you fail Him. His love for you doesn't depend on *you*, it depends on *Him*. We are used to *deserved* love, getting love that we earn. Jesus offers *undeserved* love, a love we don't deserve and can therefore never lose.

Your Life Needs Some Meddling

But you need to know this: it is a risky thing to get close to Jesus and to submit to His story. The closer we get to Jesus, the more He meddles with us. Because Jesus brought good news and was a winsome guy, people loved to be around Him. But He constantly meddled with their lives!

Meddling is interfering, messing around, changing plans, getting into someone's business, and rearranging. Westerners are independent, individually minded people who don't like people messing with our stuff and our business. We want to live life our way.

A recent *USA Today* article by Cathy Grossman titled, "More Americans Customize Religion to Fit Their Personal Needs," cites George Barna, the widely respected researcher, declaring that "America is headed for 310 million people with 310 million religions." Barna goes on to say, "We are a designer society. We want everything customized to our personal needs—our clothing, our food, our education . . . now it's our religion."[2] In the past this wasn't the case. There were different religions, sure, but people didn't customize beliefs to their own individual preferences.

Even today, though, people still want Jesus; they just want Him as an add-on, an accessory. They want to customize Jesus to fit their preferences. If we can get a pair of shoes to match every outfit, a suit for every occasion, a cell phone case that expresses our personality, and a car that makes a statement, then why not accessorize our lives with a little bit of Jesus?

This looks different for different people. My friend in Denver says that what people want in Denver is: "a Subaru, a spouse, a golden retriever, 1.5 kids to fit in your bungalow, a ski pass, and maybe a little bit of Jesus."[3] For others it might be a career, to make a name for one's self, stock options, and the chance to stay busy and fit, with the hope that Jesus can get in where He fits in. For many here in Silicon Valley, it's the chance to be a D. I. N. K. —Double Income, No Kids—with a nice, neat Jesus that doesn't disturb their peace and security.

Here's the problem with that. Jesus won't let us get away with it.

Remember in Chapter 1 when I told you a little about my climb up Mt. Rainier with the guys? I got very cold while climbing Mount Rainier. I didn't say to the mountain, "All right, I've had enough. My toes are about to fall off. Why don't you go ahead and warm up a bit?" All I could do was bundle up even more. When I got tired I didn't say, "Okay, mountain, enough is enough. Level out a little, already. My legs are killing me." No, all I could do was suck it up, dig in with my crampons, and keep climbing. The mountain didn't submit to my preferences, I had to submit to the mountain. Jesus doesn't adjust to us, and He doesn't submit to our whims. We adjust to Jesus and submit to Him. Jesus is King, not an accessory.

Why is it that Jesus can meddle with people like this? Because He has knowledge no one else has. Jesus knows everything about us. He knows stuff about us we don't even know. He sees our blind spots: the places where guilt lives and festers, those parts of the heart and parts of our story where we either can't or won't look because the regret, shame, and wounds run so deep, it's too painful to look at. Jesus knows *all* that.

Without recognizing we have those blind spots, there can be no relationship with Jesus. We have to recognize that we are broken people. And once we recognize that, we need to realize that entering into a relationship with Jesus means He will never leave us alone. He will turn our lives upside down, inside out, and poke His disturbing, healing finger into all those deep, dark, scar tissue–covered places.

Jesus doesn't come asking if He can hang out with us. He commands us to follow Him. He has total authority and will settle for nothing less; He won't settle for being an accessory, an add-on, or a peaceful accompaniment to a nice life. No, He will rule and He will meddle. To accept Jesus is to accept His total authority in your life.

All of us already have rulers in our lives, someone or something that sits in the place of highest authority. We need to ask ourselves, "Who is the real king of my life?" Is it some notion of worldly success? Is it money, achievement, fame, a dream home, a perfect body, a certain lifestyle, a human relationship, events from the past, or desires for the future? To give someone that much power is a frightening thing. We've all seen what happens when power is abused. But there is one person, one king, whose authority in our life we can trust.

In our most honest moments we all want someone to come into our lives and meddle with us. We want disturbance. We want someone to change us and set us free. We want someone to fix what's broken. All this meddling by Jesus is for our *good*. He's a good king. He accepts us as we are, knowing every detail of our story—the good, the bad, and the ugly. He enters our lives and meddles with our stories in order to set us free.

If your God can't disturb your life, then you don't have a real God.

The Burden That Frees

It's easy to think of God as a cop—an authority figure watching our every move, eager to pull us over when we screw up, write us a ticket, make us pay our fine, let us go, and watch closely to see if we screw up again. This is especially true for people who grew up in a religious context of some kind. But in the Bible, Jesus is constantly talking about freedom.

One of the most powerful statements of the freedom Jesus offers is found in the gospel of Matthew. In Matthew 11:28–30 Jesus says, "Come to me, all who labor and are heavy laden, and I will give you rest. Take my yoke upon you, and learn from me, for I am gentle and lowly in heart, and you will find rest for your souls. For my yoke is easy, and my burden is light."

A yoke was a wooden framework that farmers laid on the shoulders of animals (especially oxen), to steer, direct, and control them. It was big, and it was heavy. In the ancient world, teachings and belief systems were also known as yokes. A person would take on the "yoke" of a certain rabbi or religious system. This meant they would submit to it, follow it, and be "steered" by it. These kinds of yokes could be just as big and heavy as the wooden frames on the back of the ox.

Every one of us has a yoke. We all have a controlling influence, a system of belief, something that steers and controls us. And many of these yokes are exhaustingly heavy to bear. We submitted to this yoke, we put it on because we thought it would make life easier and better, but it has instead worn us down.

What is it that Jesus said about His yoke? "My yoke is *easy* and my burden is *light*." Easy and light! That's what we yearn for, and it's only found under the yoke of Jesus.

Yoked

To understand this, though, we need to know what it is that Jesus is asking us to take on. What is this yoke He lays on our lives that is so easy and light?

When Jesus calls us, He's not tampering with the outskirts of our lives; He goes straight for our very identities, the very core of who we are. Look back again to Mark 1:16–20, which we also explored in Chapter 1.

> Passing alongside the Sea of Galilee, he saw Simon and Andrew the brother of Simon casting a net into the sea, for they were fishermen. And Jesus said to them, "Follow me, and I will make you become fishers of men." And *immediately they left their nets and followed him.* And going on a little farther, he saw James the son of Zebedee and John his brother, who were in their boat mending the nets. *And immediately he called them, and they left their father Zebedee in the boat with the hired servants and followed him.*

What happened when Jesus approached these men? Jesus said "follow," and these two groups of men left behind their livelihood and their family to follow Him. Simon and Andrew left behind "their nets," their vocation as fishermen, to follow Jesus. James and John "left their father" to follow Jesus. In that culture a person found their identity in their work (similar to our culture) and in their family ties (less similar to our culture). These first disciples of Jesus left behind what had been their source of identity, the place where they found their worth and value, in order to follow a new king.

Jesus took priority over their identity. He didn't seek to destroy their vocations or their families or do anything at their expense, but He did demand that He be the source of identity. Just like these men, we all find identity in something. They were fishermen and sons in a culture where your vocation defined you and family was everything. We are the type of people who work really hard to *be* something, to make it. Some of us succeed. Some of us fail. Either way, we are dissatisfied. The identity we sought was a disappointment. The yoke we put on was too heavy and wearisome. Jesus lifts this identity-seeking yoke from our shoulders and gives us the one yoke, the one identity, that sets us free.

Climbing Mount Rainier involved many highlights, but do you know what the best part was? Finishing the climb. When we reached the bottom of the mountain, the end of the trail, I tossed off my helmet, dropped my forty-five-pound backpack, took off my heavy boots, stripped off layers of wet clothes, and sat down on a curb in the sunshine. I felt free! That's what meeting Jesus is like. The heavy burden (yoke) of sin falls off. We find the relief of peeling off layers of shame and tossing aside old guilt.

Lightness and freedom take over because Jesus offers, and is, the true story. That yoke, the heavy burden we carry, is the weight of pursuing and living a false story. It is a story built around the pursuit of false happiness, pursing idols—those things we dedicate our lives to that we aren't meant to dedicate our lives to. The things that become idols can be good things (like money, success, or a relationship), but when we turn these good things into ultimate things, into the center that our life orbits around, we find ourselves enslaved instead of free.[4] The longer we live that story, the heavier that yoke gets as the weight of dissatisfaction, guilt, shame, and brokenness piles up. Instead of this weight, this messed-up story, Jesus opens the way to the true story with His easy yoke.

Repent and Believe

In response to this good news, all people, believers and not-yet believers alike, are called by Jesus to do two things: repent and believe. Repenting and believing is what you do when you first become a follower of Jesus, and it's what you continue to do as you move forward in following Jesus.

Repent. Repent means to make a U-turn, a total change of direction. Lose your pack, your burden. Make a change of direction and change of mind—instead of following false masters, follow Jesus.

Believe. Enter into a new life, governed by the true King by acknowledging His lordship. Profess that you believe in Him, His Spirit, and His Son, and that you believe in the power of His death and resurrection in your life.

Jesus will not stop—He will keep attracting you to Himself and meddling in your life until He gets your attention, until you either repent and believe or choose to reject Him forever. It's up to you. I urge you to stick with this unfolding story long enough to learn more about Jesus so you can make a very informed rejection or acceptance of Him.

"I'd be homesick if I knew where home was."
—J. J. Connolly[1]

· · ·

"If I find in myself a desire which no experience in this world can satisfy, the most probable explanation is that I was made for another world."
—C. S. Lewis[2]

· · ·

7

ACT 5:

HOME

In the fourteenth century, Dante Alighieri wrote a famous book called *Inferno*. It's about hell, and at the time, it was fairly scandalous. In his story, he filled hell with living people he thought were corrupt, mostly leaders of the Roman Catholic Church. (You can imagine some people weren't real thrilled about that.)

Dante describes the gates of hell quite vividly, the place where one descends into hell. At these gates is an inscription: "Abandon hope all ye who enter here." That is the perfect way to describe hell, a place without hope and without any bright future. Hope has abandoned hell.

We live in a time in history when many people are abandoning hope in this life too. For probably the first time in American history, many people are saying children will be worse off than their parents. For the first time, the belief in the promise of progress has waned. Even politicians recognize this trend. When Barack Obama was campaigning for the presidency in 2008, he built his entire platform on this idea, this one word: hope. But when I talk to people in my city, I hear a repeated theme. It doesn't matter whether they are thirty years old or fifty or seventy, the theme is the same. Life didn't turn out the way they hoped. There is nothing quite like the acute pain of unfulfilled hope.

Before his own death, Steve Jobs, when talking about death and his thoughts on hope and the afterlife, had this to say: "I like to think that something survives after you die. It's strange to think that you accumulate all this experience, and maybe a little wisdom, and it just goes away. So I really want to believe that something survives, that maybe your consciousness endures . . . but on the other hand, perhaps it's like an on-off switch. Click! And you're gone. Maybe that's why I never liked to put on-off switches on Apple devices."[3]

That's pretty grim. He *wants* to believe there's life on the other side of the grave, but he doesn't really think there is. That idea of life as an on-off switch doesn't offer much hope to live by, and this from a hero of the current generation of Americans. I guess it makes sense, then, that we are abandoning hope. We're not in hell yet, but we're awfully close to "Abandon hope all ye who enter here."

But we want to hope. We want there to be something more to this life. In a recent interview with *Esquire* magazine, William Shatner, the man who played the iconic Captain Kirk from Star Trek and heroic figure to my parents' generation, also expresses his hope that there's something more than a mere on-off switch: "There's an alternative to oblivion. But I don't think it's conscious. We're all embers from the same fire. Our ember winks out, we're ashes, we go back to the fire. I like that image. There has to be a unifiying theory. I think there is a continuity of some kind, that my love for my wife will go on past the death of my body."[4]

Captain Kirk, the man who dared us "to boldly go where no man has gone before," the best he can hope for the future is an unconscious afterlife where, as ashes, we go back to the same fire we originally came from. That's a small hope.

What's the True Story?

Is this generation's diminishing hope the right view of the world? Is it based on the true story, or is it something else entirely? Does the Big Story offer anything to remedy the hopelessness of this age? I think it does. We are now in Act 5: Home, the final act of the story. Take a look at Revelation 21:1–8. It's the very last book of the Bible and, like all the best stories, tells of the hero's victory and a happy ending.

> Then I saw a new heaven and a new earth, for the first heaven and the first earth had passed away, and the sea was no more. And I saw the holy city, new Jerusalem, coming down out of heaven from God, prepared as a bride adorned for her husband. And I heard a loud voice from the throne saying, "Behold, the dwelling place of God is with man. He will dwell with them, and they will be his people, and God himself will be with them as their God. He will wipe away every tear from their eyes, and death shall be no more, neither shall there be mourning nor crying nor pain anymore, for the former things have passed away."
>
> And he who was seated on the throne said, "Behold, I am making all things new." Also he said, "Write this down,

for these words are trustworthy and true." And he said to me, "It is done! I am the Alpha and the Omega, the beginning and the end. To the thirsty I will give from the spring of the water of life without payment. The one who conquers will have this heritage, and I will be his God and he will be my son. But as for the cowardly, the faithless, the detestable, as for murderers, the sexually immoral, sorcerers, idolaters, and all liars, their portion will be in the lake that burns with fire and sulfur, which is the second death."

Why Hope?

Our house has a nice lawn, and my family loves to play in it. We have picnics, play ball, and have loads of fun on this gorgeous green grass. It's great. The lawn flourishes because of the water it gets twice a day from the sprinkler system and the warm California sunshine. Throughout the year, though, the weather shifts. There are stretches where there is less sun, and during these times we find it less valuable to run the sprinklers. During these stretches with less sun and less water, the grass begins to wilt. It goes dormant and doesn't grow. We choose not to spend the money and time on it, so for that portion of the year our grass sits lifeless.

Hope is the sunshine and sprinklers of your life. It's what makes you grow and thrive. Without it, you won't flourish. There's a saying that goes, "Human beings can live forty days without food, four days without water, and four minutes without air, but we can't live four seconds without hope." Hope is more than a good idea; hope keeps us alive.

It's not hard to make the argument that the most dangerous thing in life is losing hope. People have died because of the loss of hope, because of a broken heart. A doctor will examine the body and find it healthy—no disease, no weakness. The body gave up life because it just wasn't worth living anymore. Hope may be our most powerful possession.

Before we go on, we must define what "hope" is. Hope is the belief in a better future, a reason to move forward in life. Proverbs, a book in the center of the Bible that's loaded with basic wisdom for living life, says, "Where there is no vision, the people perish" (Proverbs 29:18 KJV). If there is no vision of a brighter reality ahead, people perish, their spirits fail them. But hope isn't just a noun; it's also a verb. You don't just have hope, you have to hope. It is a choice, a pursuit, a taking of action.

False Hope

What are those areas of your life that cause you the most distress or pain? It might be a family situation or something at work or maybe being out of work altogether. Whatever it is, take ten seconds and imagine that it will improve. Imagine that the problems will be resolved, the pain will dissipate, and it will be better. What will that look like and feel like? Didn't it feel good to imagine that? I bet you felt just a bit better, even if it was brief.

But that little exercise might have been dangerous. The only thing more dangerous than no hope is false hope. No hope leaves you floundering. False hope takes you to a height of what seems like flying and then plunges you back to the hopeless reality of pain and perishing.

Victor Frankl was a Jew and a survivor of a Nazi concentration camp, and he came to the conclusion that those who were able to survive the concentration camps were those who kept hope. But he said the most dangerous thing was to have false hope. He knew a man in the camp who arbitrarily set a date of March 30, 1945, as the day when the Jews would be liberated and rescued. He clung to this made-up, self-created hope for months leading up to March 30. Even as things got worse and worse in the concentration camp, he held fast this date. The day came and went, and there was no liberation for the camp. The next day, March 31, 1945, the man died. Victor Frankl concluded that he died because he had placed all his hope in the wrong place. His false hope failed him and ultimately killed him.[5]

The True Story of Hope

What we need is a story about the world, a worldview that will give us true hope. We need a story that will not let us down when all the false hopes crumble. Because they surely will. This whole book is about that story, the Bible's story, as one single narrative in five acts—God, Creation, Rebellion, Rescue, Home. These same five acts can be applied to other worldviews as well, to understand their stories and what they say.

Act 1: God, asks the question, "Who is God?" Every worldview answers this question differently. The Big Story answers this in Genesis 1:1, that there is one God, a Trinitarian God, who loves to be God and enjoyed perfect community before creating any of us.

Act 2: Creation, asks the question, "Who am I?" Every worldview has an answer to this. In the biblical story the answer was found in Genesis 1 and 2. I am a person created in the image of God, and He said I am "very good." Other worldviews require that you earn your identity.

Act 3: Rebellion, answers the question, "What's wrong with

me and the world around me?" Our story says that the problem is we are all sinners. Some have been outwardly rebellious prodigals, going our own way and trying to rule our own lives. Others have been outward rule keepers and "good people," but with rebellious, prideful hearts that want nothing to do with God and His grace. We are what's wrong with the world, our sin.

Act 4: Rescue, answers the question that is the most pressing for so many hearts: "What's the solution to all the pain in the world?" The Bible's story tells of Jesus, God's own Son, sent by God to pay the price of God's judgment on people for our sins, even though He Himself never sinned. His pure sacrifice created a way for us to be restored to God again, to have the relationship that was broken by sin.

And now we are in Act 5: Home, which asks the question: "What do I hope for, and where am I going?" Again we turn to the story of the Bible to see where it takes us and to find out what is next in the grand narrative. We do this because only Scripture, only Christianity, tells the story that truly gives hope, lasting and deep hope, to get us through this often painful life.

Remember, the Big Story is something different from religion. Religion is all about what *you* must do. The Big Story is not about religion, but about the gospel, about the good news of what God does for us. This is critical to understand when we talk about hope.

> Christianity is the unreligion. It turns all our religious instincts on their head. . . . The ancient Greeks told us to be moderate by knowing our inclinations. The Romans told us to be strong by ordering our lives. Buddhism tells us to be disillusioned by annihilating our consciousness. Hinduism tells us to be absorbed by merging our souls. Islam tells us to

be submissive by subjecting our wills. Agnosticism tells us to be at peace by ignoring our doubts. Moralism tells us to be good by discharging our obligations. Only the gospel tells us to be free by acknowledging our failure. Christianity is the unreligion because it is the one faith whose founder tells us to bring not our doing, but our need.[6]

Hope hinges on God, not on you. Put down this book. Take a deep breath. See if you can muster up hope from the recesses of your heart. You cannot. We must come to God with our need, our dependence. Our relationship with God doesn't depend on our doing but on our need. Our hope hinges on God, not us. We need not try to muster bigger hope but rather trust a bigger God.

Hopeful for Home

Place matters far more than we think it does. We live in an age, the Internet age, when we can do everything remotely and connect anywhere at the press of a button or the swipe of a touch screen. It's easy to think that where we work and where we live don't matter geographically because we are "connected" to the world. But location does matter. Our world may be more connected today, but people are no less homesick.

In *The Last Battle*, the last book in The Chronicles of Narnia series by C. S. Lewis, the unicorn named Jewel finally reaches heaven and exclaims, "I've come home at last! This is my real country. . . . This is the land I've been looking for all my life."[7] That's what it means to know God, to meet Him on the other side of death. It is to come home. To arrive at a *place* where everything is put back together, made new, at peace and whole.

Have you ever been homesick? When I was a teenager, I would

go off to camp or on a trip, and I would miss home. At times, it wasn't even just a twinge. I mean *really miss* it. Home was that safe and comfortable place where I fit and knew my way around. I just wanted to go back there. The Bible tells us that we are born homesick. We come into the world with a longing for home. This world, in its current state, isn't our home. We grow up feeling an emptiness and a craving, even if we don't always recognize it. Innately we recognize that there is a home somewhere out there for us, and we yearn for it. That is what Revelation 21 tells of. Our life right now is only the beginning of the Big Story. Home is where the story really starts.

The New Home

Heaven is not what some of us grew up hearing about in church. It's not the distant land of flannel graph clouds, harps, and halos. It's not some ethereal otherworld of floating spirits and angel wings. What the Bible actually teaches is that heaven will come down to earth. Home will come to us. The Bible doesn't give the mechanics, the timing, or too many details, but it's clear that there will be a new heaven and a new earth, and it will happen here on our planet. It is described as a "New Jerusalem," a holy city for all God's people.

There is another way to think about this five-act story. Think of it as a series of four chapters: Good, Bad, New, and Perfect. The story starts good, but it's not yet perfect. God's creation is flawless, but it is not yet the complete perfection He ultimately has in store for it. Things are good, but heaven and earth are still separate realms. Earth doesn't yet reflect heaven. Then things go bad. People sin and rebel. The good that was is taken from near-perfect to broken and bad. But Jesus comes to rescue, and by Him all things are made new. A new covenant is born and a new hope is realized for the redemption of the world. Finally, perfect arrives when heaven and earth come together upon Christ's return. God's people will dwell with Him in His presence in the new heaven and new earth, the new and perfect home.

The presence of God is a central theme that runs through the Bible. It is woven throughout the stories as people seek to get into His presence, to dwell with Him, to be near Him. But throughout the story, that can never happen. There are always barriers, separation between God and people, and God put them there. He is too holy, too pure, for sinful people to be near, so He protects them. First there was the tabernacle, then the temple with the Holy of Holies, where only the designated high priest could go once a year to encounter the presence of God. No one else could get that close to God or they would die.

Then God sends His Son, Jesus, who is the full revelation of who God is. Colossians 2:9 tells us that in Jesus, "the whole fullness of deity dwells." He is fully God and fully man, and He offered a taste of what it means to be in the presence of God. And now, here at the end of the Bible's story, we finally arrive, fully in the presence of God. Home is where we can be in the presence of God.

Now, let's return to Revelation 21. It begins with a loud voice from the throne. The Bible's story began with a voice, and now it is ending with the same one. "Behold," it says, "the dwelling place of God is with man" (v. 3). Wow. We don't even have categories for this. It is entirely different than anything experienced throughout human history and anything else in the Bible's narrative. It truly means to dwell with God, to live with Him. We will be in God's presence.

There are no words to adequately describe this in print or any other way. All we can do is read and wonder. We will be *with* God.

We (all who have believed in this Big Story) will *see* God. Yes, we have the Holy Spirit in us right now, helping us to know God and experience Him to the degree we are able. But we have never come face-to-face with the living God. We've never been able to. Our imperfection would be burned up in His holiness. But on that day, we will be there. We will be face-to-face with God.

We serve a God who is driven to dwell with His people. He is driven to dwell with the rebels who have run from and rejected Him. He is driven to dwell with the legalists and rule keepers who try to earn His favor. He even wants to dwell with all those who think they could be Him or replace Him. This is the ultimate purpose of the grace God gives us: to bring us home to live with Him.

Many Voices, One Understanding

Imagine that voice from the throne. If you are an American reader, you're likely imagining that the words will be in English. But why would that be? All peoples will be there, every tribe, tongue, and nation. People will be there from every culture and every era of history. This voice will speak to all of us, even languages that are long since dead and forgotten. Will it be some heavenly language that we don't yet know or speak? We can't know how, but we do know that God will make Himself known and understood to everyone.

Not only that, but all people will be able to understand each other on that day. Maybe we'll get to meet some heroes of the faith. I want to talk to Martin Luther and ask him all about the Reformation; he spoke German. I want to talk to King David, the greatest Israelite king; he spoke Hebrew. I don't know how this will work, but on that day, it will. All believers will know the voice of God and be able to speak with one another.

Sadness Comes Untrue

Now as we are all conversing and hearing and understanding, we hear an even greater promise. "He will wipe away every tear from their eyes, and death shall be no more, neither shall there be mourning nor crying nor pain anymore, for the former things have passed away" (Revelation 21:4). What are these former things? What does this mean?

In *The Return of the King*, the culminating book in The Lord of the Rings trilogy by J. R. R. Tolkien, Sam Gamgee is seeking hope, seeking solace, and he asks this question: "Is everything sad going to come untrue?"[8] That is the question we have all asked, maybe out loud or maybe deep in our hearts. It is one of the questions of a heart longing for our true home, away from all this sadness. And here we have our answer, a resounding "YES!" All that is sad in this world will come untrue.

If the resurrection is true, if Jesus Christ really is the Son of God, if He really did come to earth, die for our sins, and rise again from the grave, then yes: everything sad will come untrue. We have this to hope for, that the former things will pass away. And that sadness is one of those former things.

Think about what is promised, what will be done away with. God will wipe away every tear. Every tear you have ever shed (or ever held back, for you more stoic ones) in your life over pain or grief will be gently wiped away. Death will be no more. Can we even imagine such a thing? Death defines life as we currently know it; everything dies. But not in that day. There will be no more aging, no more decay, no more disease, no more accidents or tragedies leading to death. Mourning will cease. All the heaviness of soul you bear, all the weight of sadness that hangs around your heart, all that will be lifted—never to return. And there will be no more pain. As the character Westley so memorably says in the movie *The Princess Bride,* "Life is pain."[9] And he was right, but no more. Once you arrive in this home, you will not be able to get hurt or give hurt. All your sadness will come untrue.

More than an Upgrade

A couple of years ago, I upgraded my TV during football season from standard definition to high definition. It's a striking change, so much cleaner, crisper, and clearer. What's happening on screen seems so much more real. Sometimes we envision the new heaven and the new earth this way, like upgrading to a high-definition life. It'll be a cleaner, crisper, nicer experience.

This is so far from reality. We lack even the categories for how much better life will be on that day in that place. Our feeble minds are incapable of processing the realities of our new, true home until we get there. Rather than an upgrade, it's more like someone who has spent their entire life imprisoned in Antarctica. The days are short and blistering cold; the nights seem endless and are somehow even colder. He is all alone. He is withering away to nothing. Then, out of the blue, he is inexplicably rescued. On the long journey, he is barely conscious, but when he comes to, he finds himself on the beaches of Santa Barbara, warmed by a friendly sun. He is served whatever food and drink he fancies and is surrounded by caring people, friends who will not leave him. And he is promised that it will never end, but get better every day as he regains his health, a true health he didn't think was possible.

This is no mere upgraded life with more clarity and a nicer experience. It is a transformed, utterly morphed, entirely new life in which everything sad is untrue. An upgrade would not be worth staking your life on, but this new life will be worth every bit of it.

All Things New

We have now arrived at the pinnacle of the promise, the best part of the entire passage, and the pinnacle of the whole Bible's story. This is the resolution to all the conflict, the fruit of all the labor, the ending to every quest. It is the greatest, most hope-giving promise in all the universe. "Behold," God says, "I am making all things new" (Revelation 21:5). All things. New.

God is going to redeem all things. All the hard things in life, all the bad things, all the difficulties, all the brokenness—all of it will be redeemed and made new. Some will be redeemed by being done away with altogether and some will be redeemed by being repaired and restored. Revelation 21 goes on to tell us that God is the Alpha and the Omega. These are the first and last letters of the Greek alphabet and signify that He is the beginning and the end. He is before our beginning and after our end. God stands outside of time and history—not distant, but not bound by it. He was present before time started being recorded and He will be there for all eternity, beyond when time can be measured any longer. And it is because of this that He can take all of life, all of history, and make it altogether new.

C. S. Lewis said this, "Some mortals say of some temporal suffering, 'No future bliss can make up for it,' not knowing that Heaven, once attained, will work backwards and turn even that agony into a glory."[10] That is what our new home, this new heaven and earth, will do. It will work backward and turn all your agony into glory. Somehow, in God's power and wisdom, He has ordered the universe in such a way that the bliss you experience with Him on the other side of the grave will be greater, precisely because of the things you suffered in this life. That's worth banking your life on.

As a kid, I remember watching my grandmother quilt. I would watch and wonder. There she sat with a pile of scraps, a ball of yarn, and a seemingly undecipherable pattern of thread. How could anything worthwhile come out of that mess? But as I kept watching, over time, I would see the thread pattern becoming clearer and those scraps pieced together as the quilt grew. The colors would pop and contrast, and in the end there would be this tapestry of a quilt. That is what God is doing in this world and has been for all time. We just see a pile of scraps and a mess of thread that means nothing and looks chaotic. It is disordered and ugly, but in heaven we will be able to see the perfectly patterned quilt of God's handiwork. It will take all eternity to completely grasp His work, but we will see how He was working backward, from scraps to beauty, from broken to redeemed.

Rescue and the Second Death

There can be no heaven, though, without God doing something with evil. That is the paradox of judgment. Our hearts long for all the promise of this passage, but what is to be done with the evil in the world, the evil in our hearts, and with people who refuse to bow the knee to Jesus, the true King of the universe? God cannot leave that unaddressed, for He is perfect and holy and cannot tolerate evil in His presence.

The Bible is clear that every person will experience resurrection, whether or not they follow Jesus. Everyone will die (unless Christ returns prior to their death). This is the first death. And upon Jesus' return, every person, living and dead, will be resurrected. That is to receive a new body. This is not some horror movie with grotesque creatures or wispy, wailing spirits rising out of the earth. It is a transformation from our present, mortal state to a state of bodily perfection and immortality. But on that day, some people, those who reject Jesus and refuse to worship Him, will experience the second death.

The very last verse of this passage describes hell. "But as for the cowardly, the faithless, the detestable, as for murderers, the sexually immoral, sorcerers, idolaters, and all liars, their portion will be in the lake that burns with fire and sulfur, which is the second death" (Revelation 21:8). God must judge sin in order to be both holy and just. So how is it that this dilemma is solved since all of us are unholy?

God solved this dilemma for us in Jesus, as we saw in the last few chapters. Jesus bore God's judgment, He was the substitute for sinners, so that all who follow Him can have this new, true home. The simple reality of the story is this: there are two people who can pay for your sin: either Jesus pays for your sin, or you pay for your sin. Either Jesus pays for you and you receive His grace, or you reject His grace and pay fully for your sin in the second death. And that is why all people are resurrected with immortal bodies, either to spend eternity in God's presence or eternity separated from His presence. Either you are bought by God, or you pay the infinite debt against an infinitely holy God forever and ever.

All who trust Jesus have this to hope for—that we will not

experience judgment because Jesus was judged in our place. But how can this be? The list of sins listed in verse 8—cowardliness, faithlessness, detestability, murder, sexual immorality, sorcery, idolatry, lying—pretty well covers everyone. All of us have done some of this stuff. We are all guilty, and these are the descriptors of those folks who will inhabit hell. So how can we have hope?

But this verse is not merely describing having done these sins; it is describing those who refuse to repent. To repent is to turn away from sin and turn to Jesus, to acknowledge your need for a Savior who can face the judgment for you. Those who continue to hold to their old life of sin and spurn Jesus are those who face the second death. This is a call to repent, to turn to Jesus with all that you are.

Sin is the problem. Hell is the consequence. Jesus is the answer.

Just Drink

How is it we can be sure we have this hope? It sounds so good. It tugs at the heart. But what must we do to have it? Just one thing: drink. God says, "To the *thirsty* I will give from the spring of the water of life without payment" (Revelation 21:6). See how simple God's conditions are? All we must do is drink—acknowledge our thirst, acknowledge our need. All we need is need. If you're thirsty, you qualify. Drink your fill of this life and hope.

When I played football in high school, I did this thing for a couple of years where I refused to drink any water during practices or games. I thought refusing water would make me tougher and would prove my strength. In reality it just proved my stupidity. The refusal to drink was pure pride. A person can't live without water, but I so much wanted to be "tough" that I let pride stand between me and what my body needed. Many of us are like that with God. We think: *I don't need grace. I'm good enough and strong enough on my own. I can make it through life and earn God's favor all by myself.*

But heaven is for thirsty people, people who come to God and drink. Christianity is the unreligion because it is the only one in the world that does not demand our doing but our need. There is no earning it.

I love that old hymn by James Proctor, "It Is Finished." The last verse says this:

"Lay your deadly 'doing' down—
Down at Jesus' feet;
Stand in Him, in Him alone,
Gloriously complete."[11]

There is a reason why the hymn says *deadly*. All our doing, on its own, leads to death. We think it earns favor with God, earns a ticket to heaven. But all it earns us is hell. It is truly deadly. God's love is for sinners, for people who know they need rescue. God's love doesn't work on anyone else.

The Math of God

I remember when my son Cru learned to add. It happened basically overnight, and he learned it all on his own. We would see him sitting at the kitchen table and his fingers would be flying as he figured out the sums. We'd toss some math problems at him, "Hey, Cru, what's three plus four?" and he'd work it out and excitedly announce "Seven!" He was so proud of himself. That's how math works. Three plus four will always equal seven.

But God's math isn't like that. He works differently. To add up to being good enough for God, we need to realize that we offer nothing. We add nothing to the equation. It's not some of my good plus some of God's grace equals heaven. We are always a zero in the equation of salvation. Philip Yancey calls this "the atrocious math of the gospel."[12] In this atrocious math, we must realize that all we bring is need. We bring nothing, a zero, and God provides everything to make us righteous. He provides forgiveness, justification, and a new future through Jesus.

We get to live like the children of a billionaire. The child of a billionaire doesn't have to do anything to earn his parents' money. He is an heir, and an heir simply has to be part of the family. All those riches will come precisely because he is a child of the billionaire and for no other reason. And so it is with God. All we must do is be His children, and we will inherit immeasurable blessing.

Bright Future

There's a song by the band Timbuk3 from back in the eighties called, "The Future's So Bright I Gotta Wear Shades." If you are a Christian, this is true for you. Timbuk3 might not have known exactly what they were singing, but they described the hope of a Christian pretty well. Your future is so bright, you can't even imagine it.

You are going home someday. That longing in your heart will be fulfilled. All this mess and pain and ugliness will be quilted by God into something beautiful. He will make all things new in our new, true home. No other story says this.

Everything sad will come untrue. Perhaps the best way to express this future that awaits all who trust in the Big Story is expressed again in Tolkien's novel *The Return of the King*, as Sam sees his friend Gandalf after thinking him dead:

But Sam lay back, and stared with open mouth, and for a moment, between bewilderment and great joy, he could not answer. At last he gasped: "Gandalf! I thought you were dead! But then I thought I was dead myself. Is everything sad going to come untrue? What's happened to the world?"

"A great shadow has departed," said Gandalf, and then he laughed and the sound was like music, or water in a parched land; and as he listened the thought came to Sam that he had not heard laughter, the pure sound of merriment, for days upon days without count. It fell upon his ears like the echo of all the joys he had ever known. But he himself burst into tears. Then as a sweet rain will pass down a wind of spring and the sun will shine out the clearer, his tears ceased, and his laughter welled up, and laughing he sprang from his bed.

"How do I feel?" he cried. "Well I don't know how to say it. I feel, I feel"—he waved his arms in the air—"I feel like spring after winter, and sun on the leaves; and like trumpets and harps and all the songs I have ever heard!"[13]

STORY CONTRAST (HOME VS._____): The Big Story says that all of human history is headed toward home or hell—toward an eternity of bliss with God or an eternity of brokenness apart from God. What stories do people around you believe about where human history is headed? In what ways does the Big Story make better sense out of the future to come?

ACTION STEP: Think more about eternity. Most of our problems and pain would drastically shrink if we viewed our troubles in this world through the lens of eternity. Thinking more about eternity will actually make you more fruitful in this life.

RECOMMENDED READING: *Who Will Deliver Us?* by Paul Zahl (Wipf & Stock, 1983). It may have just been the season of life I was in, but I slowly read this very short book last summer, just a page or two a day, and it gave me a brand-new appreciation for God's grace and the unchanging hope we have in Him.

"Only when you know how to die can you know how to live."
—J. I. Packer[1]

• • •

*"Twenty years from now you will be more disappointed by
the things you didn't do than by the ones you did do. So throw off
the bowlines. Sail away from the safe harbor. Catch the trade
winds in your sails. Explore. Dream. Discover."*
—Mark Twain[2]

• • •

*"Is it absurd to believe that one human being, a tiny dot on a tiny planet,
can make a difference in the history of the universe?"*
—Philip Yancey[3]

• • •

8

LIFE

I once read about a nursing home in Texas that conducted a study with incoming residents for about ten years. As elderly people, usually in their eighties or nineties, were admitted into the home, they were asked one question: What is one thing in your life you wish you would have done differently?

About three-fourths of those who answered said something along the lines of, "I wish I had taken more risks."[4] And here in this final chapter, you too must answer these questions. What are you doing with your life? What does it mean to live an unwasted life?

In the last chapter we saw what the future holds, what home looks like, where sadness will come untrue, and where all things will be made new. But we aren't there yet. We live in a time between Rescue (Act 4) and Home (Act 5). We live in between Jesus' first coming and His second coming. This is the time God deemed best to give us life. So how do we live this gift of a life without wasting it? How do we steward this gift?

The Bible has much to say about the way we are to live. But we often miss it, or at least miss the big picture and get fixated on smaller details. This missing, big-picture doctrine is the epilogue to the Big Story. It tells us how to live now while we await our homecoming.

A Parable

Jesus uses a story, a parable, to explain to His disciples what it means to live an unwasted life. It is the parable of the ten minas (we'll get to what a "mina" is). Jesus tells this story while He is on the way to Jerusalem for the last time. His entire ministry has been building up to this time; He is on His way to die. Jesus loved to teach through parables, through story. Stories open up new ways of thinking and paint a picture of life that brings to light aspects that might otherwise go unnoticed. Learning from stories requires a different sort of listening, but when we hear what a story is saying, it can be more powerful than any other form of learning. And Jesus was using every bit of this power to give His followers final important instructions before He left them.

> As they heard these things, he proceeded to tell a parable, because he was near to Jerusalem, and because they supposed that the kingdom of God was to appear immediately. He said therefore, "A nobleman went into a far country to receive for himself a kingdom and then return. Calling ten of his servants, he gave them ten minas, and said to them, 'Engage in business until I come.' But his citizens hated him and sent a delegation after him, saying, 'We do not want this

man to reign over us.' When he returned, having received the kingdom, he ordered these servants to whom he had given the money to be called to him, that he might know what they had gained by doing business. The first came before him, saying, 'Lord, your mina has made ten minas more.' And he said to him, 'Well done, good servant! Because you have been faithful in a very little, you shall have authority over ten cities.' And the second came, saying, 'Lord, your mina has made five minas.' And he said to him, 'And you are to be over five cities.' Then another came, saying, 'Lord, here is your mina, which I kept laid away in a handkerchief; for I was afraid of you, because you are a severe man. You take what you did not deposit, and reap what you did not sow.' He said to him, 'I will condemn you with your own words, you wicked servant! You knew that I was a severe man, taking what I did not deposit and reaping what I did not sow? Why then did you not put my money in the bank, and at my coming I might have collected it with interest?' And he said to those who stood by, 'Take the mina from him, and give it to the one who has the ten minas.' And they said to him, 'Lord, he has ten minas!' 'I tell you that to everyone who has, more will be given, but from the one who has not, even what he has will be taken away. But as for these enemies of mine, who did not want me to reign over them, bring them here and slaughter them before me.'" (Luke 19:11–27)

As we read, the following truths become clear. The nobleman in the parable is Jesus Himself. He is the King, and He is announcing that although He came and accomplished what He intended, He would be leaving soon for a long journey. But more than that, Jesus wanted to make it known that His departure would not be permanent. He is coming back, and this story is to prepare His listeners for that second coming. This is the overarching purpose of the parable.

As we read further, we see the king give one mina each to three of his servants. A mina was a coin worth about three months' wages for a laborer, so it would be the equivalent to several thousand dollars in today's currency. But along with this sum, the king gives a command to the servants: "Engage in business until I come." That is the big message, the take-away command from this story. Servants of the King are to take what has been given to them and use it, grow it, and maximize its fruitfulness until He comes back.

Return on Investment

And at the end the king does return. He comes back demanding results. How did the servants do with that mina he left them? He provided valuable resources; what have these servants done with them?

The first servant created a tenfold return on the one mina investment. He turned three months' wages into thirty, and the king is pleased. He rewards the servant with a position of greater responsibility. So too, the second servant succeeded to the tune of a fivefold increase—more than a year's wages. The king fairly rewards him as well with a position of increased responsibility.

But the third servant? He brought the original mina to the king. He had hidden it in a handkerchief and now handed it back with nothing earned. The king's response is quick and furious. He accuses the servant of failing to do even the simplest thing to make profit—put the mina in the bank to earn minimal interest. He then takes the mina and gives it to the first servant, the one who had earned the most significant profit. He takes from the one who accomplished nothing and gives to the one who accomplished most.

Occupy

When Jesus tells His disciples this parable, He could have framed the story any way He wanted to. He could have emphasized certain ideas and given certain commands. But He gave only one. Notice, though, what Jesus did *not* say.

He didn't say, "Engage in church activities until I come." He didn't say, "Engage in Christian subculture until I come." He didn't say, "Pull back from life in your city and figure out how to be a good usher at your church." No, He says, "Engage in business."

For those of you reading this book who are not Christians but who have been moving closer in that direction as you've been trying on the Big Story, you must beware of this: many Christians privatize their faith. Unfortunately, some Christians can be really good at doing this, at taking their faith in God, their servanthood to the King, and making it a private part of their lives. So often, people mistake Christianity for a gnostic or dualist viewpoint on faith, a faith that's separated from everyday real life. Some Christians go to church, read their Bible, and believe in God, but the rest of their lives—how they spend the bulk of their week—is totally separate from following Jesus. Don't do this. If and when you place your faith in Jesus, I want you to live a big and complete life of following Him. The Big Story calls for this, not for a compartmentalized, small faith.[5]

Jesus' command here is clear: "Engage in business." I love how the King James Version of the Bible translates that phrase:

"Occupy till I come." Jesus tells us to *occupy* this world until He comes back. We have lost the powerful vision of being given the gift of a life. We've been given opportunities and resources to engage and occupy the world for Jesus' name, fame, and glory until His return. We have settled for private faith with a little bit of church and a little bit of prayer.

Abraham Kuyper, the Dutch theologian, politician, and journalist (now *that's* an example of occupying the world as a Christian), famously said, "There is not a square inch in the whole domain of human existence over which Christ does not cry 'MINE!'"[6] Christ looks over every inch of the universe and declares it to be His. He owns it all. He is sovereign over all. And it is from this ownership and sovereignty as King that He commands us to occupy, to engage in business. And He is gracious to give us resources to do so. "God's story reveals that God is the King, the world is his kingdom, and we are his stewards."[7]

All of life is spiritual, not just church or "quiet times" or prayer. Life is not just about church on Sunday; it's about Jesus on Monday. Our mission of obedience should be to make an impact for Jesus in our communities, in our places of business. For me and my church, that place is Silicon Valley, and that is how I lead and encourage the people of Garden City Church. We state the mission of our church in eight words: *Making disciples to impact the city for Jesus.* When someone joins our church, they don't join a mere meeting or gathering of people, they join a mission. Here in Silicon Valley, an area that's significantly influencing the rest of the world, I want to unleash our people to pursue their vocations at Apple, at Google, or as teachers, landscapers, stay-at-home moms, bankers, or whatever it is God has called them to do in such a way that they impact our city in the name of Jesus. And not just a temporal impact, we want an eternal impact. This is what the local church should be—a community of diverse people, deployed throughout the city, with diverse callings, networks, and strengths, on a mission to change their city.

On Assignment

Nearly everyone in the United States knows about D-Day. In the spring of 1944, 160,000 Allied troops were massed in southern England to prepare for an invasion of France. On June 6, 1944, this army stormed the beaches over a fifty-mile span of Normandy, France. They staked their claim through a hail of bullets and artillery shells and occupied the beachheads. Their success created the way into the Western Front so that the Allies could take back Europe from the Nazis.

When those men stormed the beaches, every one of them had an assignment, a specific job. There were ground troops, pilots providing air cover, paratroopers going in behind enemy lines, sailors transporting the troops, artillery men and gunners bombarding the German positions, medics and corpsmen providing first aid, engineers, and many more. Each of them had a specific assignment as part of this mass mission to regain Europe. And every follower of Jesus has an assignment in this world as well.

Each Christian plays a role in occupying this beachhead for the glory of God and the expansion of His kingdom. What is your assignment? What has the King asked of you in your city, your neighborhood, your workplace? You have a part in occupying the world for Jesus; what is it?

So many Christians live as if life is simply for biding time, waiting, and avoiding sin until Jesus comes back. But we are not called to passivity. A few sentences in the New Testament, 2 Peter 3:11–12, provide a staggering message about the purpose of our life and calling. These sentences read, "What kind of people ought you to be? You ought to live holy and godly lives as you look forward to the day of God and *speed its coming*" (NIV). We are to live holy and godly lives. That is a high calling—no surprise in the context of following Jesus. But that next phrase is stunning. We are called to play a role in speeding the coming of the day of God. That's the outworking of our faith in Jesus and calling from Jesus. Somehow, someway, what the church does, what all of us believers in the Big Story do, contributes to the second coming of Jesus. This commission to "engage in business" is a tremendous responsibility. It's no mere time killer until our lives end or Jesus returns. It is a life's work, a life's purpose, and it matters.

Have we lost sight of the fact that God gave us life? This wasn't just happenstance. Life is a gift from the Creator of the universe, a gift that we are supposed to do something with. We were created to be shapers of history through our words, our actions, our work, and our dreams. I have been assigned to plant and pastor a church. That is my assignment at this time in history. I am to rally the people of my church and the readers of my books to know *their* assignments and to go after those assignments.

Brothers (and Sisters) on a Mission

In the American church, women vastly outnumber men. The statistics clearly show it, and it's not hard to see by scanning the pews at the average church on a Sunday morning. There is a man problem in the church. Men simply don't see where and how they belong in the church. The church has lost connection with them by misrepresenting its mission. It's as if the message to men in many churches is, "Grow up and aspire to be an usher someday." Men are to aspire to be stuffed suits with nice smiles in religious buildings, and it has no connection whatsoever to what they devote their lives to for fifty or sixty hours every week.

Band of Brothers was an HBO mini-series about Easy Company of the U.S. Army's 101st Airborne Division. They are a diverse bunch with varied backgrounds and personalities, but as the story progresses, they gel as a unit and come together as a team. They are on a mission to fight evil by defeating the Nazis and to protect the interests of their homeland. Through these battles and missions and trials, they coalesce from a group of disparate warriors into a true band of brothers. This is what church should feel like for men. It should feel like a squad of brothers on a crucial mission, not like being stuffed suits passing a plate. In many ways, the church has succeeded in being this for women, but men need to know and feel it too.

To have a body of men and women on a mission like this would truly change the world. Look around. See the violent crimes that are being committed. Look at the broken families and the parentless children. Look at the sex trade industry. Men are responsible for the bulk of this mess. I want the church, especially the men of the church, to own their responsibility to do something about this mess. We have a mission to occupy culture, and we can begin to do something about it. Leave behind the notion of a privatized Christian faith, and join a band of brothers on this mission to change the world.

An Unwasted Life

There are two quotes that describe so well what it means to live an unwasted life, to fulfill our purpose and mission. Pastor and theologian John Piper is known for his passionate preaching and pointed writing about finding joy in God. He says, "Whatever you do, find the God-centered, Christ-exalting, Bible-saturated passion of your life, and find your way to say it and live for it and die for it. And you will make a difference that lasts. You will not waste your life."[8]

Francis Ford Coppola is best known for directing *The Godfather* and *The Godfather: Part II*. He isn't much of a theologian and may not even be a Christian, but his insight into living the right kind of life is profound. He said, "I was always a good adventurer. I was never afraid of risks. I always had a good philosophy about risks. The only risk is to waste your life, so that when you die, you say, 'Oh, I wish I had done this.' I did everything I wanted to do, and I continue to."[9]

These two quotes from strikingly different men balance and complement one another. Coppola tells that "the only risk is to waste your life," and Piper tells exactly what a wasted life is—that which fails to "find the God-centered, Christ-exalting, Bible-saturated passion of your life." Have you found your way to live for Jesus? What will you say when you get to the nursing home someday and are asked what you would change about your life? What risks will you regret not taking? And what fears are keeping you from serving Jesus?

If you are a teacher, your mission is to teach for the glory of God. If you are a lawyer, your purpose is to do justice for Jesus. If you are a craftsman or artist, your mission is excellence in your field to reflect the great Creator. If you are a homemaker, your assignment in this occupation is to raise your children to know and honor God so that there is a next generation to occupy even further. The kingdom calls all of us to mission, to fulfill the call we have and thus live a fulfilled life with no regrets.

Rewards

Everything we do with our lives has eternal effect and will lead to either eternal reward or eternal punishment. Lately I have been learning a lot about rewards. One of our sons got some cavities, so my wife started researching ways to prevent and remedy this. One night she ran across a recipe on the Internet for a concoction that involves cod liver oil and some other ingredients, and it's supposed to reverse the effects of tooth decay, as well as offer other health benefits. I guess this is what happens when someone stays up too late on the Internet. So over the past months, I have been a regular imbiber of cod liver oil. And it is nasty. It's what a floating, bloated, dead carp in some backwater of a river would taste like. But I keep taking it because I believe in the health benefits. I believe there will be a reward in the long run.

Jesus promises rewards too, except His are big and eternal. Christians can be afraid to talk about rewards sometimes for fear of eclipsing grace, but the rewards are real. How we live our lives on this earth will lead to rewards in the new earth. There are greater rewards in heaven for those who steward this life well. The main motive driving the lives of believers is grace, the message of the gospel, that undeserved favor of Christ to save us from ourselves. But reward must influence us too; it should give us motivation and hope. The first coming of Jesus, the forgiveness gained by His death and resurrection, should shape our hearts and lives. Christ's second coming with its glory and rewards should set the vision for our lives.

We must always be asking the questions: What am I going to do in the in-between time? What has God called me to do with my life to advance His kingdom and speed His coming? We must live with the first coming fresh in our mind, knowing that the second coming could be tomorrow. We live in the freedom of grace and the hope of heaven, doing the unique work God has called us to do. Indeed, "There is something that we have been created to do that no one else has been made to do in the way that we do it."[10]

Punishment

In the parable of the minas, there was one servant who did not obey the master's command to engage in business. All that he had been given was stripped away. Those who fail to do anything useful with the resources and opportunities God has given them will fall under His displeasure too. To shirk a duty like this, to ignore a clear command, is an indication that someone is not a believer in Jesus at all, so we must vigilantly evaluate ourselves. Are we obeying? Are we stewarding what God has given us?

This servant was condemned by his own words. He says, "Lord, here is your mina, which I kept laid away in a handkerchief; for I was afraid of you, because you are a severe man" (Luke 19:20–21). The King responds with a terrifying response: "I will condemn you with your own words, you wicked servant! You knew that I was a severe man" (Luke 19:22). In short he says, "If you had truly believed what you just said, you would have taken action and obeyed me." The servant is simply making excuses for his actions, trying to flatter the king. The problem is that he doesn't even know his king.

So often, those who fail to do anything fruitful with their lives make excuses. They blame circumstances. They blame finances. They blame their current family situation or their family of origin. Hard things will happen. They happen to everyone. Life is difficult; we live in a hard world. But this is true for everybody. We don't get to play the victim card. That won't fly with the King. Especially not when Jesus Himself came into this hard world, endured every hard thing, and accomplished His mission to the glory of God without flaw. Theodore Roosevelt articulated this theme well, the danger of living life on the sidelines, in his speech "Citizenship in a Republic," which he delivered at the Sorbonne in Paris, France, on April 23, 1910:

> It is not the critic who counts; not the man who points out how the strong man stumbles, or where the doer of deeds could have done them better.
>
> The credit belongs to the man [or woman!] who is actually in the arena, whose face is marred by dust and sweat and blood; who strives valiantly; who errs, who comes short again and again, because there is no effort without error and shortcoming; but who does actually strive to do the deeds; who knows great enthusiasms, the great devotions, who spends himself in a worthy cause; who at best knows in the end the triumph of high achievement, and who at the worst, if he fails, at least fails while daring greatly.[11]

Obstacles

What keeps us from what God tells us to do in this passage? Mostly self-imposed obstacles. There are any number of reasons we find to not fulfill the mission we are given. I am going to highlight three of them.

Private Part Christianity

Everyone has private parts. We don't talk about them in public. We keep them hidden. They're not for anyone to see or know anything about, except for our spouses. And we certainly don't flaunt them.

The problem arises when people treat the Big Story like this, and many do. We treat God like this. We keep Him private, hidden away. It's awkward to talk about Him in public, so we don't share Him or the stories of our faith with people. Because our Christianity is hidden, it has no effect on our relationships, our neighbors, or our places of work.

But Christians don't just do this individually. It's as if we have a secret-handshake agreement with others to hide Christianity as a group. We are excellent at coming up with parallel institutions, totally separate ones, from our culture. We have our own schools, bookstores, music, clothes, even coffee mugs and picture frames. We don't engage culture. (There are, of course, wonderful exceptions to this. But by and large the American church is better at retreating from culture than engaging culture.) The very definition of being a Christian is to be a missionary, to make our faith outward focused. But instead we hide it away like a private part of life.

Decaffeinated Grace

In the past, what I am referring to as "decaf grace" was known as cheap grace. It is believing in grace, claiming it for your own, without a changed life. That's not real grace. Real grace leads to change. Ephesians 2:10 says, "For we are his workmanship, *created in Christ Jesus for good works*, which God prepared beforehand, that we should walk in them." And this comes right on the heels of one of Scripture's greatest declarations that people are saved by grace, not works, in verses eight and nine. We are not saved *by* works, but rather *for* them. "Saved by grace, not works" is a message I would die for, but we must be saved by a faith that works. We are saved by faith alone but that faith is never alone. True faith transforms.

Many people slurp up the message of grace, but there's no kick to it. But when we drink in real, true grace, change will begin to happen in a hurry. Cheap grace is like decaf coffee: it can look the same, it can smell the same, it can even taste the same, but that's all that's the same about it. When you drink it, nothing happens.

God gives grace so that our lives will be transformed. It's not because He needs our good works to help Him out, to do Him a favor, to gain Him anything. He has what Scripture calls "the cattle on a thousand hills" (Psalm 50:10). We might say He has all the Bentleys and mansions in the world. As Martin Luther said, "God doesn't need our good works, but our neighbor does."[12] So God gives real, caffeinated grace that enables us to work hard and make an impact in this world.

School

The third obstacle might sound a little funny. It doesn't affect everyone, but it has a subtle yet powerful effect on many. It is the reality of our schooling system. Schools have taught us how to do good, standardized testing. They have taught us to live life like it's an assembly line of sorts—every question has an answer, everything has its place, life is a system, and we can work it out. It's data in, data out. We are conditioned to think like there is an answer key to solve all our problems, to give us the answers to all of life.

When we were born God didn't give us an answer key. He didn't make clear what your gifts are or what your assignment in life would be or how best to live it. He has given broad instructions, principles on how to live and glorify Him. When the king in the parable gave the mina to the servants, he didn't say, "Go invest in real estate," or "Check out these stock options." He said, "Engage in business," and so it is with us.

Seth Godin, an entrepreneur and author in New York, says that instead of training us in standardized testing and robotic-like thinking, school ought to teach people two things: how to lead, and how to solve interesting problems.[13] That's what Jesus lays out in this passage. He provides an opportunity to take the lead, to solve the problems of being in business in a broken world. Albert Einstein believed school should stimulate the imagination and creativity. Jesus says that here too. It takes imagination and creativity to explore how we can best engage in God's business in our world.

The first commandment in the Bible, from way back in Genesis, is to "be fruitful and multiply" (Genesis 1:28). That sounds very much like "engage in business" or "occupy." God was telling Adam and Eve, back in the garden, to be like the fruit trees all around them by producing much fruit and good for their world. So must we in our world. George Washington Carver put it well: "No individual has any right to come into the world and go out of it without leaving behind him distinct and legitimate reasons for having passed through it."[14] We are to speed the second coming of Jesus by figuring out our unique way to impact this world for Jesus.

Play Big

Too many of us play small with our lives. I played football in high school. I eventually became a good football player, but my freshman year I was the worst player on the team. The absolute worst. My coaches would put me in the game in the fourth quarter when my presence on the field could have no effect on the outcome of the game, either because we were winning by so many points or losing by so many points. I made two tackles all year, both by accident. I was over six feet tall and 120 pounds, which means that as a high school freshman, I had the body of a female supermodel.

I often found myself playing small, not just because I was fairly small, but because I held back and didn't give it my all on the field. I didn't believe I could make much of a difference. This is what we do with life; we don't give it all we have. Sometimes this is driven by false humility, the mindset that says, "I don't want to show all my strength or talent since that might show somebody up." For others it might be fear of failure. This is the idea that if we put everything we have into something we are called to do and fail at it, then we have *really* failed miserably. But if we only give 90 percent of ourselves to it and fail, we can always say, "If only I had given 100 percent, I would have succeeded." Playing small gives us an out, a layer of self-protection against failure. Playing small is what we do when we live afraid, when we focus on self-protection instead of living for our King. Writer Marianne Williamson puts it well: "Our deepest fear is not that we are inadequate. Our deepest fear is that we are powerful beyond measure. . . . *Your playing small does not serve the world*. There is nothing enlightened about shrinking so that other people won't feel insecure around you. We are all meant to shine, as children do. We were born to make manifest the glory of God that is within us."[15]

Unfortunately, most people play small instead of playing big. We hold back, instead of pouring out our lives for the benefit of others. People quote poet Henry David Thoreau as saying: "Most men lead lives of quiet desperation and go to the grave with their song still in them." Thoreau never said this. This is actually a combination of something Thoreau wrote and something poet Oliver Wendell Homes wrote:

"The mass of men lead lives of quiet desperation."[16]
—*Thoreau,* Walden

"Alas for those that never sing, But die with all their music in them."[17] —*Holmes,* The Voiceless

Once we reach Home, there will be plenty of grace for us, whether or not we went to the grave with the music still in us, but it honors Jesus to go to the grave playing the song He's given us to play.

Jesus is calling us to play big, to take the life He's given us and maximize every bit of it. He is calling us to take the grace and the story He has given and play big. We are to position our lives for maximum fruitfulness. To avoid doing this is a sin. It's easy to name sin as lying or lusting or stealing; it's just as much of a sin to waste our lives. It is a sin to hold back, to play small.

We must not undersell God's ability to use us. There is a story about the opening of Disneyland. It was just a few weeks after Walt Disney's death. At the ribbon cutting, one of the honored guests said to those around him that it was such a shame Walt couldn't be there to see it. Michael Vance, who had taken over operations of Disney, responded, "He did see it. That's why it's here."[18] Walt

Disney had a vision of what could be, and that's why it came to be.

To change our cities, our cultures, it will take more than a few churchy people. It will take a church of people following the call of God. It will take a church that plays big, that has a vision for change and allows God to put us to work in it. We are to be a church that Satan is scared of. Every morning when we get out of bed, Satan should shudder at what we might do that day for Christ's kingdom.

Playing big means that we must *play*. We cannot be a church of spectators. We are on a mission to make disciples, and to overcome and inspire the world for our King. Nobody on a mission can idly stand by and watch, not the faithful servant or the band of brothers or any one of us. This is a life of action, obedience, and purpose. This world needs an active Christianity, a strong Christianity. It needs us to play big.

A. W. Tozer once said, "Anything He did anywhere else He will do here; anything He did any other time He is willing to do now; anything He ever did for other people He is willing to do for us!"[19] Will you believe this? God is more committed to the Big Story than we are—He cares more about making a difference in and through your life than you do. Let us live with faith that God is God and we are not. His job is to be God, our job is to play big with the life, grace, and resources He's given us while we live in this exciting in-between place in the Big Story. He has great purposes for all of us.

Slaying Dragons

Since we have been exploring the greatest story ever told and our place in it, it is only right to leave you with a story. It is from the classic tale of "Saint George and the Dragon."

One day St. George rode throughout the country. Everywhere he saw the men busy at their work in the fields, the women singing at their work in their homes, and the little children shouting at play.

"These people are all safe and happy. They need me no more," said St. George.

"But somewhere perhaps there is trouble and fear. There may be someplace where little children cannot play in safety, some woman may have been carried away from her home— perhaps there are even dragons left to be slain."

"Tomorrow I shall ride away and never stop until I find work which only a knight can do."[20]

There are still dragons to be slain in our world. So we must go forth, engage in the business of slaying them, stay on mission, and play big. God has given us so much. He's given grace. He's given the gospel. He's given us life temporal and He has offered life eternal. He has given us our stories, our talents, our passions, and our strengths so we can go forth to find work that only we can do.

We long to hear God say, "Well done, good and faithful servant" (Matthew 25:21). He will say that to any who have a relationship with Jesus. But we give more pleasure to God if we honor Him with all of life. Look ahead to that nursing home. What story will you tell when you get there? Will it be one of regret, of emptiness, of a wasted life? Or will you tell of slain dragons and kingdoms won! At the end of our days we long to tell a big story of faithfulness and fruitfulness as we followed Jesus in all things. We will all die with regrets. But, by God's grace, we can take action now to minimize the extent of our regrets.

The Big Story isn't over yet. It's far from over. Right now, while we await Jesus' return and the next and greatest chapter of the story, we each have a big role to play in shaping this Big Story. What will our contribution be?

You began this book by praying a simple prayer:

God, speak to me as I read this book.

Make Yourself more real to me.

Do something new in my life and through my life.

Now, finish this book by praying another simple prayer:

God, thank You for how You have spoken to me.

I want to play a big part in Your Big Story.

Give me clarity and give me courage as I seek to play big with my life, all for Your glory.

STORY CONTRAST (LIFE VS._____): The Big Story says that we live life in between the first and second comings of Jesus, and that the best life is a life of fruitfulness—occupying this world until Jesus comes back. What stories do people believe in your context about the current purpose of their life? In what ways does the Big Story make better sense out of the purpose behind what we do all day?

ACTION STEP: If you haven't done so already, join a great church that preaches the gospel and calls you to live a life on mission as you pursue God's unique calling on your life. Play big!

RECOMMENDED READING: *Life Work* by Darrow Miller (YWAM Publishing, 2009). This is a great book that expands what I've said in this chapter—giving great background, detail, and nuance to the big calling God places on our lives.

HOW TO RETELL OTHER PEOPLE'S STORIES WITH THE BIG STORY

Austrian philosopher Ivan Illich was once asked about the most revolutionary way to change society. He answered the question this way:

> Neither revolution nor reformation can ultimately change a society, rather you must tell a new powerful tale, one so persuasive that it sweeps away the old myths and becomes the preferred story, one so inclusive that it gathers all the bits of our past and our present into a coherent whole, one that even shines some light into our future so that we can take the next step. . . . *If you want to change a society, then you have to tell an alternative story.*[1] (italics mine)

Most of you reading *The Big Story* care about seeing change happen in the people in your city. As I seek to love and touch people in my city, I realize I must focus my energy on two main things: (1) listening to their story (2) telling them an alternative (better) story—the Big Story.

A very helpful way to do this is to use the five acts of the Big Story (God, Creation, Rebellion, Rescue, Home) as a template for understanding other people's stories and then retelling their story with the Big Story, the one story that can make true sense out of their life. What follows is a simple method for doing this.

Act 1: God

Whether it's conscious or not, everyone believes in an Act 1 part of their story. Act 1 asks the question "Who is God?" Listen for the Act 1 of people's stories—who is their god? What have they placed at the center of their life? Once you've discerned the functional god of someone's life, you can retell their story—you can tell them how the God of the Bible is a better God than whatever or whomever they currently worship. The content of Chapter 2 forms the core of this content—that there is one happy, Trinitarian God who is sovereign, wise, and good—who can be completely trusted, and who is worthy of our worship.

Act 2: Creation

Act 2 asks the question "Who am I or who should I be?" Everyone in your city is believing some sort of Act 2; some larger story is informing their sense of identity and purpose in life. Act 2 is a critical leverage point for reaching people with the Big Story. Most people's stories ring hollow here—as life goes on and beats them up, they realize that they've built their life on an unstable identity (most often, some sort of success or performance-oriented identity), and they feel aimless about the purpose of their life.

The content of Chapter 3 gives you a beautiful, better story to tell people—that they are created in the image and likeness of God, that God's words ("very good") give a person the identity they've been searching for their whole life.

Act 3: Rebellion

Everyone has an Act 3 to their story, an answer to the question "What's wrong with me and the world?" Listen closely to how people make sense of the brokenness in them and around them. You want to press for honesty here, for realism—do people really believe that the pain in this world is merely a product of people making stupid choices once in a while? The Big Story gives a far more satisfactory answer that rings true to the human experience—there is something very wrong with this world and us—it's a problem called sin and evil, a problem that we cannot fix by ourselves. The content of Chapter 4 gives you many angles for telling people the story that can make sense of what is wrong with them and this world. Talking about sin will not be popular or easy to swallow for most people, but it will ring true. The longer someone seriously examines Act 3 of their story, the more likely they are to see that only Christianity adequately explains the pain around us. Act 3 is where people can be radically humbled. Most people believe in an Act 3 that makes them the hero, rather than the problem. Most people think they can fix themselves.

Act 4: Rescue

Act 4 answers the question "What's the solution?" Again, the Big Story requires humility. Most every other story that people around you believe underestimates how bad things really are (Act 3) and therefore underestimates how significant a solution is needed. We need grace, a Savior, rescue—not self-help. Your task here is to listen closely to how people think they or someone else can fix what's broken. Gently point out the holes in their Act 4, how their heroes fail them and how there is only one hero who can rescue younger son prodigals and elder brother prodigals from a life of selfishness and brokenness. Chapter 5 gives you plenty of handles for talking about these themes.

Act 5: Home

The final act goes after hope, it answers the question "What do I hope for and where am I going?" Listen to what people long for; what is their Act 5 that they think will finally satisfy them and solve their greatest problems? The Big Story offers a vastly superior future and hope than any other story and worldview can offer. Only Christianity tells of eternal life on the other side of the grave in a world where there is no more pain or death, where everything sad comes untrue, and even the worst things that happen to us in this life are redeemed and make for a greater future bliss. Chapter 7 gives you plenty of on-ramps for talking to people about a better Act 5.

During the last two years, God has been using me more than ever before to lead people to place their faith in Jesus and experience new life in Him. It's thrilling. I'm no more equipped than you to do this. I don't have any secrets. My only "secret" is that I believe God can save anyone's life, and I work hard at listening to people's stories and telling them a better story.

If you want to change a society, then you have to tell an alternative story. The Big Story.

NOTES

Introduction

1. Robert McKee, "Storytelling That Moves People," *Harvard Business Review*, June 2003, 51–55.
2. www.GardenCitySV.com.
3. William Kilpatrick, *Why Johnny Can't Tell Right from Wrong* (New York: Simon & Schuster, 1993), 92.
4. Leslie Leyland Fields, "The Gospel Is More Than a Story," *Christianity Today*, July/August 2012, 43.

Chapter 1: Jesus

1. Leo Tolstoy, *The Devil and Family Happiness*, trans. April Fitz Lyon (London: Spearman & Calder, 1953), 52.
2. Fields, *Gospel*, 40.
3. Tim Keller, *King's Cross* (New York, Dutton, 2011), ix.
4. Jake Shears and Elton John, "When Elton Met Jake," *The Observer*, November 11, 2006. www.guardian.co.uk/music/2006/nov/12/popandrock9.
5. Mahatma Gandhi quoted in Benny Aguiar, "Gandhi and Jesus," *The Examiner*, September, 1992. http://robtshepherd.tripod.com/gandhi.html.

6. John Lennon, "How Does a Beatle Live? John Lennon Lives like This," interview by Maureen Cleave, *London Evening Standard*, March 4, 1966. www. beatlesinterviews.org/db1966.0304-beatles-john-lennon-were-more-popular-than-jesus-now-maureen-cleave.html.

7. www.faithfulchoices.com/who-is-jesus-what-famous-people-said.

8. Google Dictionary, bit.ly/VWwucF.

9. There are many excellent English translations of the Bible (the Bible was originally written in Hebrew and Greek). My favorite translation is the English Standard Version (ESV).

10. For more on the story line of cities, see my book *Why Cities Matter: To God, the Culture, and the Church* (Wheaton, IL: Crossway, 2013).

11. Kilpatrick, *Johnny*.

12. This life graph is by my friend Karen Liu, Operations Director at Garden City Church.

Chapter 2: Act 1: God

1. G. K. Chesterton, *Orthodoxy* (Rockville, MD: Serenity, 2009), 53.

2. A. W. Tozer, *The Knowledge of The Holy* (New York: Harper Collins, 1992), 1.

3. 1 Timothy 1:11.

4. Joe Brown quoted in Ben Patterson, "Our Happy God: Delighting in a Delightful and Delighted God," *Student Leadership Journal*, September 15, 2004. www.intervarsity.org/slj/article/4042.

5. Blaise Pascal quoted in John Piper, "Christian Hedonism: Forgive the Label, But Don't Miss the Truth," *Desiring God*, January 1, 1995. www.desiringgod.org/resource-library/articles/christian-hedonism.

6. Bruce Springsteen, "Hungry Heart," New York, Columbia Records, 1980.

7. C. S. Lewis, *Mere Christianity* (New York: HarperCollins, 1952), 49.

8. Saint Augustine, *Confessions*, trans. Henry Chadwick (New York: Oxford University Press, 2009), 3.

9. My favorite book on the attributes of God is the book already mentioned in this chapter, *The Knowledge of the Holy*, by A. W. Tozer.

10. The fact that God is sovereign, wise, and good radically affects how we practice gratitude with our lives. All of a sudden we see that there is more to be thankful for, that there is a larger pattern at work. Henri Nouwen puts this well: "To be grateful for the good things that happen in our lives is easy, but to be grateful for all of our lives—the good as well as the bad, the moments of joy as well as the moments of sorrow, the successes as well as the failures, the rewards as well as the rejections—that requires hard spiritual work. Still, we are only grateful people when we can say thank

you to all that has brought us to the present moment. As long as we keep dividing our lives between events and people we would like to remember and those we would rather forget, we cannot claim the fullness of our beings as a gift of God to be grateful for. Let's not be afraid to look at everything that has brought us to where we are now and trust that we will soon see in it the guiding hand of a loving God." Henri Nouwen, *The Essential Henri Nouwen*, ed. Robert A. Jonas (Halifax: Shambhala, 2009), 63

11. Bernard Bell, *Creation: Genesis 1:1–2:3, Four Sermons by Bernard Bell* (Peninsula Bible Church: Cupertino, CA 2008), 8–10.

Chapter 3: Act 2: Creation

1. Robert McKee, *Story: Substance, Structure, Style and the Principles of Screenwriting* (New York: ReganBooks, 1997), 12.

2. Fields, *Gospel*, 40.

3. Rick Warren, *The Purpose Driven Life*, Expanded Edition (Grand Rapids: Zondervan, 2012), 22.

4. Psalm 14:1.

5. Bertrand Russell, *The Basic Writings of Bertrand Russell* (New York: Routledge, 2009), 39.

6. Thomas Dubay, *The Evidential Power of Beauty: Science and Theology Meet* (San Francisco: Ignatius Press, 1999), 99.

7. Stephanie Dalley, *Myths from Mesopotamia: Creation, the Flood, Gilgamesh, and Others* (New York: Oxford University Press, 2009).

8. James Owen, "32 New Planets Found Outside Our Solar System," *National Geographic News*, October 19, 2009. http://news.nationalgeographic.com/news/2009/10/091019-32-new-planets-found.html.

9. Bertrand Russell, *Why I Am Not a Christian: And Other Essays on Religion and Related Subjects* (New York: Simon and Shuster, 1957), 107.

10. James Hufstetler quoted in Jerry Bridges, *Trusting God* (Colorado Springs: NavPress, 2008), 171.

Chapter 4: Act 3: Rebellion

1. Joel Achenbach, "A Vast Store of Information," *Washington Post*, March 12, 1999. http://www.washingtonpost.com/wp-srv/national/2000/next0312.htm.

2. Dag Hammarskjold quoted in Nancy Guthrie, *O Love That Will Not Let Me Go* (Wheaton, IL: Crossway, 2011), 18.

3. Allan Loeb and Stephen Schiff, *Wall Street: Money Never Sleeps*, DVD, directed by Oliver Stone (Los Angeles: 20th Century Fox), 2010. This line comes from Michael Douglas, playing the character Gordon Gekko.

4. Carl Sandburg quoted in Mardy Grothe, *I Never Metaphor I Didn't Like* (New York: Harper, 2008), 134.

5. Jay Newton-Small, "Steve Jobs: Silicon Valley Mourns the Death of a Founding Father," *Time*, October 6, 2011. http://www.time.com/time/nation/article/0,8599,2096339,00.html.

6. For more about my mom's story see Chapter 5 in my book *Date Your Wife* (Wheaton, IL: Crossway, 2012).

7. Jim Fitzgerald et al., "Sandy Hook Elementary School Shooting: Newtown, Connecticut Administrators, Students Among Victims, Reports Say," Huffington Post, December 14, 2012. http://www.huffingtonpost.com/2012/12/14/sandy-hook-elementary-school-shooting_n_2300831.html.

8. On the Friday of the shooting I had a sermon all ready to go for the upcoming Sunday. Once I learned of the shooting, I began to cry and pray, scrapped my finished sermon, and wrote a new message that addressed the massacre and where God fits into it. The message is titled "The God Who Suffers," and you can find it here: http://www.gardencitysv.com/#/resources.

9. Sophia Lee, "Food and Loathing," *World Magazine*, Volume 27, Number 23, November 17, 2012, 50.

10. The New Testament clearly identifies this serpent as Satan, referring to "the dragon, that ancient serpent, who is the devil and Satan" (Revelation 20:2).

11. Robert Robinson, "Come Thou Fount of Every Blessing," 1757.

12. C. S. Lewis, *The Weight of Glory* (New York: HarperOne, 2001), 178–180.

13. Stuart Walton, "The World of GK Chesterton, and What's Wrong with It," *Guardian*, January 8, 2010. www.guardian.co.uk/books/booksblog/2010/jan/08/gk-chesterton-world-whats-wrong.

14. Mark Nelson, "The Problem and Blessing of Pain," *Westmont College Magazine*, Summer 2012, 17.

15. John Stott, *The Cross of Christ* (Westmont, IL: InterVarsity Press, 2006), 326.

Chapter 5: Act 4: Rescue

1. Michael Horton, *The Gospel-Driven Life: Being Good News People in a Bad News World* (Ada, MI: Baker Publishing Group, 2009), 12.

2. J. Gresham Machen, *The Christian Faith in the Modern World* (New York: Macmillan, 1936), 57.

3. A. W. Tozer, *The Pursuit of God* (Camp Hill, PA: Christian Publications, Inc., 1993), 85.

4. About eight years ago I was deeply impacted by reading Kenneth Bailey's writings on Luke 15. He's written several books on this chapter of the Bible; perhaps *The Cross and the Prodigal* is his best book on the topic. His books made this parable come alive for me and deeply shaped my understanding of grace and the Christian life. A few years later I heard Tim Keller's sermons on this parable, which added another layer of influence. I recommend picking up Bailey's books and *The Prodigal God*, a book by Tim Keller that came out of his sermons on this parable.

5. We actually don't know if the younger son was involved with prostitutes. It is the self-righteous elder brother who later accuses his brother of wasting his money on prostitutes. Did the younger son really do this, or is this just a faulty accusation/assumption made by a self-righteous brother?

6. Kenneth Bailey, *The Cross and the Prodigal* (Westmont, IL: InterVarsity Press, 2005), 67.

7. Ibid., 82.

8. Tim Keller, "The Centrality of the Gospel." http://download.redeemer.com/pdf/learn/resources/Centrality_of_the_Gospel-Keller.pdf.

9. Robert Farrar Capon, *Between Noon & Three: Romance, Law & the Outrage of Grace* (Grand Rapids: Eerdmans, 1996), 72.

Chapter 6: Intermission

1. Martin Lloyd-Jones, *Spiritual Depression* (Grand Rapids: Eerdmans, 1965), 131–132.

2. Kathy Lynn Grossman, "More Americans Customize Religion to Fit Their Personal Needs," *USA Today: US Edition*, September, 2011. http://usatoday30.usatoday.com/news/religion/story/2011-09-14/america-religious-denominations/50376288/1.

3. This quote comes from my friend Hunter Beaumont, lead pastor of Fellowship Denver Church. Two weeks before I launched Garden City Church, I had a conversation with Hunter about Jesus and culture that made me rethink my whole approach to the way I preached on this topic and the way I wrote this book.

4. "Idolatry is by far the most frequently discussed problem in the Scriptures." David Powlison, "Idols of the Heart and Vanity Fair," *Journal of Biblical Counseling*, 13, no. 2, Winter 1995, 35.

Chapter 7: Act 5: Home

1. J. J. Connolly, *Viva La Madness* (London: Gerald Duckworth & Co Ltd., 2012), 63.

2. Lewis, *Mere Christianity*, 120.

3. Steve Jobs, "Steve Jobs talks on tape about biological dad," *60 Minutes*, CBS, October 21, 2011. http://www.cbsnews.com/video/watch/?id=7385529nn.

4. William Shatner, "William Shatner: The ESQ+A," interview by Scott Raab, *Esquire*, May 2012. http://www.esquire.com/features/man-at-his-best/q-and-a/william-shatner-interview-0512.

5. Viktor E. Frankl, *Man's Search for Meaning* (Boston: Beacon Press, 2006).

6. Dane Ortlund, *Defiant Grace* (County Durham, England: Evangelical Press, 2011), 38.

7. C. S. Lewis, *The Last Battle* (New York: HarperCollins, 2000), 196.

8. J. R. R. Tolkien, *The Return of the King: Being the Third Part of The Lord of the Rings* (Boston: Mariner, 2005), 246.

9. William Goldman, *The Princess Bride*, DVD, directed by Rob Reiner (Los Angeles: 20th Century Fox), 1987.

10. C. S. Lewis, *The Great Divorce* (New York: HarperOne, 2001), 69.

11. James Proctor, "It Is Finished!"

12. Philip Yancey, *What's So Amazing About Grace?* (Grand Rapids: Zondervan, 2002), Chapter 5.

13. Tolkien, *Return*, 246.

Chapter 8: Life

1. J. I. Packer quoted in Nancy Guthrie, *O Love That Will Not Let Me Go* (Wheaton, IL: Crossway, 2011), 15.

2. Mark Twain quoted in Laird Hamilton, *Force of Nature; Mind, Body, Soul, and, of Course, Surfing* (New York: Rodale, 2008), viii.

3. Philip Yancey, *Disappointment with God* (Grand Rapids: Zondervan, 1988), 169.

4. I regret to say that I cannot remember where I read this, but I wrote it in my notes upon reading it and haven't ever forgotten it.

5. For more on the dual dangers of privatizing your faith or secularizing your faith, see Chapter 4, "Contextualization in the City," in my book *Why Cities Matter* (Crossway, 2013).

6. Abraham Kuyper quoted in James Bratt, *Abraham Kuyper: A Centennial Reader* (Grand Rapids: Eerdmans, 1998), 488.

7. Darrow Miller, *LifeWork: A Biblical Theology for What You Do Every Day* (Seattle: YWAM Publishing, 2009), 155.

8. John Piper, *Don't Waste Your Life* (Wheaton, IL: Crossway, 2003), 47.

9. Francis Ford Coppola, "On Risk, Money, Craft & Collaboration," interview by Ariston Anderson, *99U*, January 6, 2011. http://99u.com/articles/6973/Francis-Ford-Coppola-On-Risk-Money-Craft-Collaboration.

10. Miller, *LifeWork*, 121.

11. Theodore Roosevelt, "Citizenship in a Republic" (speech delivered at Sorbonne, Paris, France, April 23, 1910). www.theodore-roosevelt.com/trsorbonnespeech.html.

12. This well-known quote by Martin Luther has been widely circulated.

13. Seth Godin, *Linchpin: Are You Indispensable?* (New York: Portfolio, 2011).

14. George Washington Carver quoted in Gary Kremer, ed., *George Washington Carver: In His Own Words* (Columbia, MO: The University of Missouri Press, 1987), 1.

15. Marianne Williamson, *A Return to Love: Reflections on the Principles of a Course in Miracles* (New York: Harper, 1996), 190–191.

16. Henry David Thoreau, *Walden* (New York: Thomas Y. Crowell & Co, 1910), 8.

17. Oliver Wendell Holmes, *The Poetical Works of Oliver Wendell Holmes: Songs in Many Keys* (New York: David Douglas, 1892), 98.

18. Michael Vance quoted in Pat Williams and Jim Denney, *How to Be Like Walt: Capturing the Disney Magic Every Day of Your Life* (Deerfield Beach, FL: HCI Books, 2004), 84.

19. A. W. Tozer, *The Counselor* (Camp Hill, PA: Christian Publications, 1993), 122.

20. William J. Bennett, ed., *The Book of Virtues* (New York: Simon & Schuster, 1993), 193.

Appendix

1. Ivan Illich, "Storytelling or Myth-Making? Frank Viola and Ivan Illich," *Proclamation, Invitation, & Warning*, July, 2007. http://procinwarn.com/counterfeit/storytelling.htm.

SPECIAL THANKS

Many thanks to my friend Barnabas Piper, who helped me on this project and made this a better book.

The End of
Our Exploring

978-0-8024-0652-1

Do we know what it means to question well?

Faith isn't the sort of thing that will endure as long as our eyes are closed. The opposite, in fact: faith helps us see, and that means not shrinking from the ambiguities and the difficulties that provoke our most profound questions.

We need not fear questions, but by the grace of God we have the safety and security to rush headlong into them and find ourselves better for it on the other side.

This book steps into the gap between non-questioning certitude and wishy-washy "dialogue for the sake of dialogue" to help us determine the role of questioning in our lives.

WHY HOLINESS MATTERS

978-0-8024-0507-4

Our generation has little or no regard for holiness. And this makes sense given our misunderstanding of:

- Sin (we view it as either inevitable or we just go with it)
- Holiness (we view it as unrealistic or we ignore it because there's no immediate payoff)
- Innocence (we view it as subordinate to "experiencing the world")
- God (we often think He'll probably let us down—just like people do)

Instead of playing the "guilt/shame" card, Tyler Braun examines Jesus' example to recognize how His way of life contrasts the world's promises.

Also available as an eBook

MOODY
PUBLISHERS

www.MoodyPublishers.com